NO
DIVISION
AMONG
YOU

NO DIVISION AMONG YOU

Creating Unity in a Diverse Church

RICHARD EYRE
EDITOR

DESERET BOOK

All photos provided by the authors.

© 2023 Richard Eyre

All rights reserved. No part of this book may be reproduced in any form or by any means without permission in writing from the publisher, Deseret Book Company, at permissions@deseretbook.com. This work is not an official publication of The Church of Jesus Christ of Latter-day Saints. The views expressed herein are the responsibility of the authors and do not necessarily represent the position of the Church or of Deseret Book Company.

Deseret Book is a registered trademark of Deseret Book Company.

Visit us at deseretbook.com

Library of Congress Cataloging-in-Publication Data
(CIP data on file)
ISBN 978-1-63993-183-5

Printed in the United States of America
PubLitho, Draper, UT

10 9 8 7 6 5 4 3 2 1

Contents

Foreword: Why Unity and Diversity Matter
RICHARD EYRE IX

Why the Lord Asks Something Beautiful and Difficult
MAURINE PROCTOR 1

Unity within the Church and Nation
THOMAS B. GRIFFITH 16

Ward Choirs: A Unity Metaphor
KATHY K. CLAYTON 27

And Unity Begat Synergy
H. CRAIG PETERSEN 34

The Gardener King
ADAM TIMOTHY 45

Rocky Ground
KIMBERLY TEITTER 52

The UNITY and Strong Families of "Nothingness"
LINDA AND RICHARD EYRE 62

The Power of Proximity
BEN SCHILATY 74

CONTENTS

The Juxtaposition of Unity and Sameness
NEYLAN McBAINE 82

Divine Diversity
MARK ESTY... 87

At-One-Ment
BILL TURNBULL 97

One Heart and One Mind
ELIZABETH HAMMOND... 105

An Optimistic Road from Contention to Unity
MELANEY TAGG... 112

Religion: How We Use It Makes a Difference
RONELL HUGH 120

Some Conclusions and Some Questions..................... 131

Notes 137

Dear Reader:

This is a book on unity and diversity. These fourteen essayists represent both—they are diverse geographically, politically, racially, orientationally, economically, and every other "-ally" you can think of; but they are also "allies" united by their strong membership commitment to The Church of Jesus Christ of Latter-day Saints.

As you progress through the book, you will come to know each of these authors. You will agree and identify with some of them very quickly and naturally, and it will be less so with others. But within this spirit of "unity with diversity," please read and think about the ones you don't initially resonate with as carefully and attentively as those with which you quickly identify.

Each essay concludes with a short section called "Discussion Questions and Personal Application." Here, each essayist poses some brief questions that will help us to not only *understand* the aspects of unity and diversity that he or she has discussed, but *use and apply* them in our everyday lives. These concluding questions can also be useful in book club discussions.

Foreword: Why Unity and Diversity Matter

RICHARD EYRE

The Problem

Church members, we have a problem.

It is a problem that centers in the United States and may be at its worst in areas where Church membership is most concentrated. It is a rapidly growing problem that was highlighted and exacerbated by the pandemic. It is a contagious, even malignant problem because it feeds on and multiplies itself. It is a personal problem that affects our outlooks, our attitudes, and our mental health. It is an institutional problem that weakens and undermines our wards and stakes. And it is a spiritual problem that can slow the work of God and threaten to impede His eternal plan of happiness.

It is the problem of division, and of the discord, dissension, dismissal, and disrespect that come with it.

It is a UNITY problem.

As a people, we are, usually unwittingly, ignoring the consistent admonitions of the Lord and His servants to avoid contention and to earnestly seek unity—even oneness. Christ Himself tells us, "If ye are not one ye are not mine" (D&C 38:27). And

FOREWORD: WHY UNITY AND DIVERSITY MATTER

in His great Intercessory Prayer in John 17, He prays that His disciples might become one as He is one with Heavenly Father. When He came to the Nephites, He was blunt in stating that "he that hath the spirit of contention is not of me, but is of the devil, who is the father of contention" (3 Nephi 11:29), and His admonition in section 136 of the Doctrine and Covenants is clear and direct: "Cease to contend one with another" (D&C 136:23). Paul backed this up in Philippians, saying, "Be likeminded, having the same love, being of one accord, of one mind" (Philippians 2:2).

Prophets of all ages have amplified the same message, that unity is of God and division is of Satan. Joseph Smith said, "Could we all come together with one heart and one mind in perfect faith the veil might as well be rent."[1] Paul put "unity of the faith" with "perfecting of the saints" as the goals of the Church (Ephesians 4:13, 12), and he begged the Corinthians "that there be no divisions among you" (1 Corinthians 1:10). More recently, President Henry B. Eyring said, "The strength of a quorum comes in large measure from how completely its members are united."[2] He added that "[Christ] was praying for us as well as His disciples when He asked His Father that we might be one."[3]

Yet we see division on every hand—politically, culturally, socially, doctrinally. We observe family members who don't speak to each other because of the different ideologies of their media sources or party affiliations, and we see people walking out on their wards because of the discomfort they feel in being more conservative or more liberal than the ward leadership—or because they don't agree with a mask policy or vaccination advice.

The real problem is that few of us think we are part of this problem. We tell ourselves that we are broad-minded and able to listen to and accept the differences and preferences of other people without judging them. But at this point, in the Church,

FOREWORD: WHY UNITY AND DIVERSITY MATTER

much of the division, discord, and tribalism, and the judging that comes with it, is inbred and systemic.

This book was written as the Church and the world emerged from the worst of the COVID-19 pandemic—which both highlighted and exacerbated these divisions. Some have suggested that we remove references to masks and vaccinations and other COVID-related controversies so that, ten years from now, the book will not seem dated. But we chose to leave them in because they illustrate so perfectly how the momentary temporal issues of the day can seem big enough to split us apart despite the vast spiritual perspectives that should unite us. The specific issues may be different ten years from now, but the effects and the dangerous divisions will be the same.

Dismissal

A friend of mine who knew about this book agreed that unity was a growing problem in the Church but certainly did not think of herself as being part of the issue. Then she had a troubling little experience. She had become acquainted with a young family that had just moved into her ward and was very impressed with them—they were bright and friendly and anxious to be involved and to contribute. She looked forward to getting to know them better. When she dropped by their home a couple of weeks later to deliver a small gift, she saw a political yard sign in their front lawn that surprised her—it was for a candidate she thought of as extreme, even dangerous, and it worried her to the point that she didn't stop or leave the gift, just drove on past, shaking her head. It was this small incident that made her realize that *she* was part of the problem. She had let one little yard sign cause her to judge this couple and to change, rather instantly and dramatically, what had been her favorable opinion of them.

Disagreement is not the problem. It is the judgment, the categorizing and stereotyping, and the wall-building that goes with it that turns differences into destructive divisions and dissension. Not agreeing with a person does not disrespect him or her, but *dismissing* that person certainly does. The moment we dismiss others—because of their opinion, their race, their sexual preference, their religion, their politics, their party, their education, their news source, their vaccination or lack thereof, their accent, their "activity" in the Church, their "faith crisis," their podcast preferences, their mask-wearing, their "conservative" or "liberal" gospel or scripture interpretations, the appearance or behavior of their children, etc., etc., etc.—we have not only disrespected them; we have judged them and separated ourselves from them, essentially rejecting them, and thus limiting or eliminating what we could do for them, what they could do for us, and what we could do together.

Ironies

The irony of this is that our wards have traditionally been a miracle of unity and acceptance of differences. We don't choose our ward membership based on being with like-minded or like-circumstance people. We go to a ward because we live within its boundaries, and the people we meet there and minister to and work and serve with are often much more diverse than our typical circle of friends and acquaintances. In many wards, we likely not only sit next to but teach or minister to or serve (or are taught and ministered to by) people that we would probably not ever encounter otherwise, let alone befriend or go to lunch with.

FOREWORD: WHY UNITY AND DIVERSITY MATTER

How, lately, has this natural, diversifying blessing of wards been trumped by our petty divisions and dismissals?

The other irony is that our glorious belief-paradigm of heavenly parents should cause something within each of us that goes beyond tolerance and acceptance and moves us toward the ultimate unity of literal premortal and ongoing brotherhood and sisterhood.

Yet somehow, someone's yard sign or skin color or vaccination status or sexual orientation seems to supersede spiritual siblinghood.

Hope

But it doesn't have to be this way. Few if any of us have consciously or deliberately made choices of division or dissension or dismissal. We slip into it. We become, subconsciously, part of a certain group, or "-ite" mindset, and within that echo chamber, whatever it is, we feel more comfortable than elsewhere, and our natural assumption that we are *right* projects "wrongness" onto those who don't match.

But the hope is that, since it comes about subconsciously, we can correct it consciously, although it may first require admitting that we are part of the problem.

Some of the essays that follow will give you different slants on the nature of the unity problem and others will suggest potential solutions. The essays range from the prosaic to the political, and from the metaphorical to the methodological. They are written by fourteen of the best thinkers and writers I know, who each see things differently than you or me or each other. They are scientists, physicians, artists, managers, PhDs, CEOs, students, and manual laborers. You will like and agree with some of them instantly, and you may be prone to dislike and disagree with others just as quickly (realizing as you do that those quick opinions you form illustrate the problem we are getting at).

These writers are called *essayists* in this book, but I think of them as friends and *collaborators*. And that word, *collaborate*, is one way to think about the solution to the problem. Can we view those with whom we disagree not as enemies or opponents or problems, but as additional perspectives, as our spiritual siblings with different experiences than our own, as *collaborators* in putting together our gospel puzzle and using it to help the world?

This collection of essays illustrates what it advocates. The makeup and diversity of the book and its authors exemplifies how different people with different opinions and backgrounds can learn from each other and find synergy in trying to understand other perspectives and viewpoints.

Diversity

My wife Linda and I, in one of the essays that you will see later in these pages, speak of the "five Ds" (also mentioned earlier in this foreword) that oppose and can undermine unity: discord, division, dissension, dismissal, and disrespect. It is important to point out here that *diversity* is *not* one of these five Ds. In fact, the only meaningful and profitable kind of unity exists across and within diversity.

That said, one of our collaborators commented: "The word *diversity* is a huge trigger to a lot of people. The argument typically goes that *diversity* leads to *division*. In many conservative circles, *diversity* is a dirty word. Perhaps that's why BYU's new diversity office is called the Office of Belonging. Should we consider swapping the word *diversity* for *belonging*?"

FOREWORD: WHY UNITY AND DIVERSITY MATTER

No one disputed this observation, but we decided to fight it rather than comply with it. The fact that "conservative circles" think one thing and "liberal circles" think another is the whole point, the whole problem, and the whole reason that we all need to learn to think another way; and when we do, we will celebrate diversity as much as, and maybe in the same breath with, unity.

In celebrating diversity and working for unity within diversity, we mirror the mind of God.

Discussion

Reading these essays will not solve the problem either for the Church or for you personally. What *will* impact the problem is *how* you read, relate to, respond to, and *discuss* their content. Just as one person couldn't have written this book alone (one person, no matter how wise and versed, can't avoid his own hidden prejudices and perspectives), one person can't read and apply its content alone either.

So let me suggest that you invite others to read it too (deliberately including diversity of orientation and opinion rather than the echo chamber of your common associations), and then meet together at least once to share your perspectives not only on the essays but on the issues they raise. Use the questions at the end of each essay and the additional more general questions in the final section of the book to prompt dialogue, and use that dialogue to expand your awareness and perspective and to identify your blind spots and to open your mind, heart, and spirit.

As we listen, discuss, and even become polite critics of each other's views, our own perspectives expand—we learn to disagree agreeably—we think again about things, and we are all the better for it.

FOREWORD: WHY UNITY AND DIVERSITY MATTER

Please enjoy that process as you read the essays that follow and perhaps as you discuss them with friends and colleagues. As you do, you will not only expand your own awareness; you will become part of the solution.

And bear in mind, as you read along, my primary point—that the things that unite us in the Church, particularly the wonderfully rarified doctrines of the Restoration—are vastly more beautiful and binding than the things that divide us.

RICHARD EYRE
2023
Park City, Utah

Why the Lord Asks Something Beautiful and Difficult

MAURINE PROCTOR

MAURINE PROCTOR, with her husband, Scot, founded and have published daily for twenty-three years *Meridian,* an online magazine for Latter-day Saints and like-minded people. They do a weekly podcast on *Come, Follow Me* and are the authors of several books. Maurine wrote the Spoken Word for the Tabernacle Choir for fifteen years. She and Scot are parents of eleven and grandparents of twenty-six.

The Lord asks something beautiful and difficult of us. To His covenant people He says, "And ye shall be my people, and I will be your God" (Jeremiah 30:22), but He adds, "Be one; and if ye are not one ye are not mine" (D&C 38:27). In fact, when we succumb to the enemy who corrupts and divides us, "all eternity is pained" (D&C 38:12).

When the Lord says, "If ye are not one ye are not mine," this is not a threat, nor a discarding of us, but simply a reality of eternal law. The Lord's presence could never be a place of contention or division. We do not break into factions in His presence, rallying around the banner of our own wounded dignity or sparring ideologies.

Thus, it is clear that a people dwelling in unity and love is not just a pleasant idea or a dream that we can never quite reach, but the very essence of those who dwell with God. This matters to Him in no small way. Zion is a people of "one heart and one mind" (Moses 7:18). In the Intercessory Prayer at the Last Supper, Jesus pled with His Father for His people, "That they all may be one; as thou, Father, art in me, and I in thee, that they also may be one in us" (John 17:21).

Living in unity, living at one, is the queen of virtues and assumes that we have learned charity and forgiveness, that we have shed resentment, disdain, and distance, that we have struggled away from offense and unfair judgment, that we have given Christ our woundedness and hurt pride.

If I were climbing toward a celestial mountain height, exercising all I had and could ever have, giving energy and breath, and, as the air grew thinner, shedding every heavy weight because its burden was too big; if, at that point of exhaustion, when I was approaching heaven's gates, trembling with my efforts, I saw someone who needed whatever help I had left to give—it may be my enemy, the one who hurt me most—that would be the person I would be asked to carry the last distance to pass the gate. That is how important unity is to the Lord.

That is so much to ask of me, but this kind of heart must be my quest.

The Sermon on the Mount

I have always been swept up in spirit by the Lord's Sermon on the Mount, given both on a green hill overlooking the Galilee

WHY THE LORD ASKS SOMETHING BEAUTIFUL AND DIFFICULT

and to the people of the new world. When the Lord shares the Beatitudes, with the various "Blessed are" statements, this actually means "oh the happiness of." He is not so much giving commandments as providing a clear description of what the happy life looks like—and it has much to do with living in unity.

One thing is clear: what Jesus describes is both beautiful and at the same time behaviorally difficult. It is not so much about what I do, but what I am, the very essence of what I have become and am becoming. I cannot achieve it by making a list and dutifully checking everything off with painstaking care. Jesus tells me that something so much more is required to transform and sanctify my very being.

He says: "Blessed are the merciful, . . . the peacemakers, . . . [and] all they who are persecuted for my name's sake." The peacemakers "shall be called the children of God" (3 Nephi 12:7, 9–10; see also Matthew 5:7, 9–10). He says, "Whosoever is angry with his brother shall be in danger of his judgment" (3 Nephi 12:22),

What is noteworthy is that in the King James Bible, this verse, "Whosoever is angry with his brother shall be in danger of his judgment," reads differently. It says, "Whosoever is angry with his brother *without a cause* shall be in danger of his judgment" (Matthew 5:22; emphasis added). That "without a cause" is not in the Nephite record—and how wise that is. How easily I can justify my fuming division from another by rationalizing that they deserve it, that my anger is justified for their horrible, disappointing, destructive behavior.

Then, of course, the Sermon on the Mount asks the most impossible thing of all. We are not just to love the easy-to-love, the comfortable, the ones who quickly and smartly identify and agree with us. (Oh, how wise they are.) No, we are to "Love your enemies, bless them that curse you, do good to them that hate you, and pray for them which despitefully use you, and persecute you; that ye may be the children of your Father which is in heaven" (Matthew 5:44–45).

What? This is surely the acid test. This is surely a bridge we must cross if we are ever to achieve unity with others, but how? How can loving our enemies possibly be done? We give up contempt altogether—even toward those who hurt us, who want to hurt us, who plot to hurt us. How can we possibly accomplish this in a world that is so angry and getting angrier, where outrage grants power?

It seems that the Lord is asking so much, because even when we have made steps forward toward living in this loving unity with those closest to us, we find ourselves surprised that frustration, dismay, and contention suddenly raise their ugly heads like thistles in a garden.

Maybe you are working toward having a family unified around Christ, but your son-in-law, who last year was in the bishopric, suddenly announces he no longer believes, and your daughter and their children are choosing to leave the Church with him. Oh no, this was the daughter who read the scriptures every day growing up. They will not participate in your family activities if you continue to pray on the food and talk about your spiritual experiences.

Or maybe you are like another friend whose daughter said, "Mother, you are such a good person. I can't believe you have such hateful ideas."

Or maybe your neighbor won't talk to you anymore because she discovered you differ politically. Or someone misunderstood what you said and won't look you in the eye anymore. Your friend begins to criticize the prophet you love and look to as a spokesperson for God.

Oh no. Oh no. Division arises out of nowhere.

The Source of Division

And yet, not out of nowhere at all. The adversary of our soul, Lucifer, that fallen angel, is the father of contention. If the Lord wants us to be at one, gathered, unified and whole, we know that, in contrast, Satan rages upon the earth, moving us to anger, hatred, division, terror, blood, and war. That old liar delights in our misery. He is the divider. When the Lord attempted to make His covenant children of one heart, Satan tempted and teased them with idol worship and violence until they were warred upon, scattered, and lost.

In his book *The Great Divorce*, which is the great divide between heaven and hell, C. S. Lewis cleverly describes hell as a great shadowed, empty city, with street after street of vacated houses, with only an occasional light here and there, extending far into the distance, to indicate that anyone lived there.

One inhabitant described why it was so empty. "The trouble is that they're so quarrelsome. As soon as anyone arrives, he settles in some street. Before he's been there twenty-four hours, he quarrels with his neighbor. Before the week is over, he's quarreled so badly that he decides to move. Very likely he finds the next street empty because all the people there have quarreled with their neighbors—and moved. If so, he settles in. If by any chance the street is full, he goes further. But even if he stays, it makes no odds. He's sure to have another quarrel pretty soon and then he'll move on again. Finally, he'll move right out to the edge of the town and build a new house."[1]

As Lewis describes the inhabitants, you understand why these streets are empty. They are blaming and self-important, they suffer from injured dignity and the need to be right, and ultimately in their quest to be better than everyone else, they become shadows of themselves, suspicious and separate.

Gathered or scattered? Unified or divided? Harmony or anger? We are swimming in these choices in multiple ways and multiple relationships every day, and since it is so clear who the covenant children want and need to be, however hard it is, the question is, "Lord, how is it done?" (Enos 1:7).

Unity must start with a human soul yearning to be united. President Russell M. Nelson was trying to help us with that when he issued a challenge on Sunday morning at general conference in April 2022. He said, "Two weeks from today we celebrate Easter. Between now and then, I invite you to seek an end to a personal conflict that has weighed you down. Could there be a more fitting act of gratitude to Jesus Christ for His Atonement? If forgiveness presently seems impossible, plead for power through the atoning blood of Jesus Christ to help you."[2]

My husband, Scot, and I took that challenge very seriously. We talked for hours about it. We couldn't find in our souls any demanding and active animosity toward anyone, but we thought we should sift deeper. Have we allowed the Lord to make us totally whole in the area of taking and giving offense? Do we have hardness toward some people, carefully hidden away in our souls, little icebergs of rejection toward others, a sense of superiority toward some and a disdain for others?

It was as we talked that I began to see both how serious and how hard being united in love really is. It is in a realm of spiritual maturity that calls for our soul's deepest spiritual calisthenics. It is not a characteristic of the natural man. It is where prophets live. It is how Christ lives. Some of the Savior's last words during His mortal ministry were, "Father, forgive them; for they know not what they do" (Luke 23:34).

Intentional Thinking

That is why, recently, a small moment spoke so loudly to my soul. Scot and I lead tours each year to Israel, where we talk about the Savior's life, and as we ended our talk in the Garden of Gethsemane, a woman came up to my husband and said a surprising thing: "I'd like to ask your forgiveness because I have been having resentful feelings toward you this last hour. I asked you when we got off the bus if you thought we needed a coat, and you said no, but it has been cold during our meeting. I really could have used a coat and I felt upset at you. Will you forgive me?"

Now, I didn't think she needed to ask for forgiveness, but I was very impressed that she had noticed those feelings of resentment in her soul and cut them off to the quick. I could see in her an intentionality of thought that allowed soul growth. She wasn't going to leap toward resentment, even for a little time, let alone dwell in it. She noticed it and stopped it.

I wanted to also be that intentional, so that I didn't go through life reflexively and quickly making judgments, piling up disapproval, feeding resentments—and all the time not knowing it because it was an invisible habit in me, a bequeathal of a fallen world. I could see that believing wholeheartedly in the majesty and importance of unity wasn't enough to be that kind of person. I had to be intentionally, actively, and prayerfully choosing love and unity.

So often we are like marbles rattling around in a box,

knocking up against each other, chipping each other in casual blows and contacts, and unaware of it.

I didn't have to wait very long to find resentment slouching into my soul. On the way home from that trip, we flew through the night and landed in Munich around 5:00 a.m. Half bleary-headed, muscles and joints aching, exhausted with that kind of dullness that is lost sleep, we juggled carry-ons and backpacks with too few hands and dragged to the first place open where we could get a bit of breakfast and sit down to eat it and unload ourselves for a minute for sweet relief. We bought our smoothies and a couple of bagels. Thankfully, about twenty-five tables and accompanying chairs were open. Balancing our smoothies as we began to unload ourselves in this sea of inviting open space, we were immediately stopped. A young man with a healthy head of blond hair and a nose ring said, "You can't eat here."

We replied, "Aren't these the chairs and tables that go with this restaurant?"

He answered, "Yes, but you ordered the wrong kind of food. Only people who order off the menu can eat here."

"But it is empty, and we are so tired," we persisted.

"You can't stay," he said. I could feel every ounce of my exhaustion rising up in silent anger as I gazed at the inviting tables and back to the young man. In my heart, I thought, he was an unfeeling idiot. Now I would have two more things—a smoothie and a bagel—to juggle in my weary walk to the faraway gate, and nowhere else to sit.

Then I saw it. I realized what I was doing. I was creating a case against him in my mind. I had judged him quickly. I had not one ounce of human kindness toward him. I was caught. I realized how far my soul had to develop yet to live in unity and love, and I asked again for the Lord to help me when I go to give

Olympic scores to the performance of the human beings around me. If I do this over small things, like our encounter at the airport, am I also prone to disunity with others in more serious matters? Obviously, there is so far to go.

Intentionality and working at being right in our minds with others is good, but clearly not enough. *Teach me how to love*, I plead. *Teach me how to be at one with thee and with my brothers and sisters*. I have to add real spiritual power to my best intentions.

How We Learn to Love

It is the Lord who teaches us to love. We must turn to Him with all our heart in the quest for the love that creates unity, because what is required is more than we can manage alone, even with good intentions. This scripture rang in my ears. "Wherefore, my beloved brethren, pray unto the Father *with all the energy of heart,* that ye may be filled with this love, which he hath bestowed upon all who are true followers of his Son, Jesus Christ; that ye may become the sons of God; that when he shall appear we shall be like him" (Moroni 7:48; emphasis added).

Filled with this love, we become unified as in Lehi's dream where he is carried away in a vision, "even that he saw the heavens open, and he thought he saw God sitting upon his throne, surrounded with numberless concourses of angels in the attitude of singing and praising their God" (1 Nephi 1:8). The word *concourses* here signifies a coming together, a flowing, an encircling of the throne of God. We are unified around the Lord. We are unified in His cause. The light that emanates from His presence fills and governs the entire universe, and we are unified because that light fills us with God at our center. He is the source of unity.

God is everywhere. "He comprehendeth all things, and all

things are before him, and all things are round about him; and he is above all things, and in all things, and is through all things and is round about all things; and all things are by him, and of him, even God, forever and ever" (D&C 88:41).

So love and unity are gifts the Lord bestows on those who spiritually yearn for them. We can be lifted and transformed through His Atonement, but we have to offer not only our willingness, but truly "a broken heart and a contrite spirit" (2 Nephi 2:7).

The Spirit utterly transforms us, through the Atonement of Jesus Christ. Our pettiness and smallness are left behind as we are sanctified and become Saints through His Atonement. Then, the Spirit, which is light, love, intelligence, and truth, delivers "the peaceable things of immortal glory; the truth of all things; that which quickeneth all things, which maketh alive all things; that which knoweth all things" (Moses 6:61).

We are given, only through God's lovingkindness, the capacity to become citizens of Zion, unified as one heart and one mind. When Zion's Camp was formed in Kirtland, the Lord said, "The redemption of Zion must needs come by power" (D&C 103:15). Some recruits thought that meant by weapons of war, but Joseph Smith taught, "By union of feeling we obtain power with God."[3]

A Hard Question

As a covenant people today, however, we live in an incredible irony. We seek to learn this love and unity in a world that teaches us war, bitterness, acrimony, and outrage. A new spirit of malevolence animates discussion in the public square as the adversary rages to sow hatred among us. Ideologies that threaten the values we hold dear are trampling over them and gaining steam.

Speech that merely used to be a difference of opinion is now

WHY THE LORD ASKS SOMETHING BEAUTIFUL AND DIFFICULT

considered a threat to someone's safety. Censorship, job loss, and canceling people become weapons to silence others. People who see things according to different ideologies are labeled with epithets by those on the other side. Extremist. Bigot. Snowflake. Racist. Homophobe. Radical. Imperialist. Killer. People on all sides of arguments see each other as existential threats. "We are losing our planet, our nation, our culture, our families—and it's your fault." Name-calling, lying, and rigging information are used to skewer people. Someone who was once a friend can turn on you quickly. How vulnerable it can be to stand for something that crosses the reigning, dominant viewpoint. Punishment may swiftly follow.

So I muse on this. Does my desire for unity and love mean I stand passively silent while truth is cast aside or freedom is dashed? If not, how can I love others while I take a stand and say what I sometimes must? In fact, wouldn't I be a little better off and a little more loving just to bow out of the current debates? Can that be an option for me or any of us?

Surprisingly, no, but it matters deeply *how* we stand for the truth in this current fray, as the gospel teaches. The world is in chaos, but if we fight in the same manner we see others do, we become part of the chaos. We heap chaos upon chaos, cast aside love and unity for war. As covenant children, we can't go there, but neither can we be silent. How do I have the power to navigate this minefield, to see in others the love that God has for them and treat them with respect, all the while worrying that the world is reeling and we are losing something of deep import?

Elder Neal A. Maxwell warned prophetically:

> Irreligion as the state religion would be the worst of all combinations. Its orthodoxy would

be insistent and its inquisitors inevitable. Its paid ministry would be numerous beyond belief . . .

Your discipleship may see the time when religious convictions are heavily discounted. . . . This new irreligious imperialism seeks to disallow certain of people's opinions simply because those opinions grow out of religious convictions. Resistance to abortion will soon be seen as primitive. Concern over the institution of the family will be viewed as untrendy and unenlightened.

In its mildest form, irreligion will merely be condescending toward those who hold to traditional Judeo-Christian values. In its more harsh forms, as is always the case with those whose dogmatism is blinding, the secular church will do what it can to reduce the influence of those who still worry over standards such as those in the Ten Commandments. It is always such an easy step from dogmatism to unfair play—especially so when the dogmatists believe themselves to be dealing with primitive people who do not know what is best for them. It is the secular bureaucrat's burden, you see.[4]

President Gordon B. Hinckley said, "The Book of Mormon speaks of the Gadianton robbers, a vicious, oath-bound, and secret organization bent on evil and destruction. In their day they did all in their power, by whatever means available, to bring down the Church, to woo the people with sophistry, and to take control of the society. We see the same thing in the present situation."[5]

It seems that the call from prophets who live in a tumbling

world, then, is to speak the truth or be silently complicit in what happens. As covenant people, we do this while first and foremost seeking to live in the unity God has asked of us. Is this impossible? On our own it would be.

Only He can show how to see the hearts of those who deeply disagree with us and start there in our discussions. The Spirit can teach us where and how to talk, how to live not by lies, but still in love.

Meanwhile, Nephi, speaking of our day, says, "I, Nephi, beheld the power of the Lamb of God, that it descended upon the saints of the church of the Lamb, and upon the covenant people of the Lord, who were scattered upon all the face of the earth; and they were armed with righteousness and with the power of God in great glory" (1 Nephi 14:14).

If the power of the Lord descends upon the Saints of God, He will show us how to navigate these wonderful and difficult times.

We can stand for truth, and at the same time, we can grow in unity, and though this sounds extremely tricky, the Lord will show us how. The peace of Christ abolishes enmity. The Atonement of Christ was meant to bring us at-one not only with God but also with His children.

Meanwhile, in my rough-and-tumble world, I can remember some ideas:

- I will pray every day to be filled with love.
- I will seek to really see others in their wholeness, rather than reduce them to their contrary opinions or their petulance. I will not dismiss someone as a person if I don't like his or her ideas.
- I will have trust that the Lord can solve broken things.

- I will not expect that it's another person's job to make me comfortable, to like me, to sympathize with me, or to affirm me. All these are gifts from others, not duties that they must do to earn my approval.
- I cannot control how other people respond to me.
- I will be quick to forgive and will rely on the Lord to show me how when it seems just too hard.
- I will not treat other people as objects who are to be useful to me or discarded.
- I will not let passing judgment become a silent habit that I don't know is happening.
- I will actively seek the light that unifies us.
- I will actively seek beauty for ashes.

I have known this unity I speak of again and again in my life, when, filled with the Spirit, I can see, with love, every person around me and happiness just suffuses my being. It happened recently at church. Our bishop stood and asked us to pray for members of our ward because so many were suffering with challenges. I knew some of those challenges, but certainly not all. A friend whose heart had been attacked when he had COVID, a young woman who had a tumor on her pancreas and couldn't eat, a wayward child who had thrown away the treasures of the gospel his parents had tried to teach him. A thousand quiet tears could flood us.

We were together in this. We knew.

I thought, though the details differ, we are all on the same perilous, joyful, stretching journey, and everyone needs a shoulder to lean on. The mountain is steeper than we thought. *Pray*, the bishop asked. Pray for each other. Unity filled my heart with joy. I would give anything to bless these my friends. And I felt the

WHY THE LORD ASKS SOMETHING BEAUTIFUL AND DIFFICULT

Lord say, "That's what I'm asking. Everything. What I will return to you is more."

Discussion Questions and Personal Application

1. What is so beautiful about unity, and why might the Lord insist upon it for His people?
2. Why is unity so behaviorally difficult to achieve? Why would the Lord ask us to love our enemies?
3. What kind of division have you seen erupt in your life? Where did it come from? How might it have been stopped?
4. Trying to think intentionally about loving others, despite how difficult they sometimes are, is good—but not enough. Where must we turn to obtain the gift of love that allows us to be unified?
5. Can you create unity in this world by merely being quiet in the face of those who would destroy you and the values you hold dear? What is expected of you in these difficult situations?

Unity within the Church and Nation

THOMAS B. GRIFFITH

THOMAS B. GRIFFITH served on the U.S. Court of Appeals for the D.C. Circuit and is currently a lecturer on law at Harvard Law School and a Fellow at the Wheatley Institute at Brigham Young University. He and his wife, Susan, live in the countryside of Loudoun County, Virginia.

As Latter-day Saints, we are called to be agents of reconciliation and unity within the Church and within the larger society in which we live.

Within the Church

Jesus's prayer for His disciples at the Last Supper, described in John 17, is an oft-cited passage of scripture among Latter-day Saints, typically used to reinforce Restoration insight that the Father and the Son are separate beings with a unified purpose.

But in our eagerness to make a persuasive point about the nature of the Godhead, we overlook the very purpose of the prayer. In the moments just before facing His greatest trial, an ordeal in which He, "the greatest of all, [would] tremble because of pain, . . . bleed at every pore, and . . . suffer both body and spirit" (D&C 19:18), Jesus gave voice to His deepest yearning and prayed to the Father that His disciples "all may be one . . . [so] that the world may believe that thou hast sent me" (John 17:21). In other words, according to Jesus Himself, the unity of His followers would be the most important witness of His divine mission that they could offer the world.

And yet the political tribalism that dominates American society today has worked its way into the Church and blunts the force of that witness. As Elder Lance Wickman, emeritus General Authority Seventy, recently observed, "Too many of our people have traded their religion for their politics."[1] It seems that we haven't learned the point Hugh Nibley stressed that politics in the City of Man is not the primary work for followers of Christ. Our main task is to build the City of God that will then work to transform the world. We have a phrase for that project in the Restoration: building Zion.[2] It's vital that we not confuse our calling to build Zion, which is grounded in revelation, with our politics, which are not. Patrick Mason notes the danger of failing to make that distinction: "The kingdom of God doesn't map onto party platforms; when Jesus returns it won't be to a party convention. Political argument is good, but if our partisanship compromises our Christianity, we need to reconsider which bags we are carrying and for whom."[3] St. Thomas More, the sixteenth-century Catholic martyr, understood the distinction. Executed by Henry VIII for placing his allegiance to church above country, More's last words were, "I die the King's good servant, but God's first."[4]

What Elder Wickman sees taking place in the Church has been noted by others about American Christianity at large: "As Christianity's hold . . . has weakened, ideological identity and fragmentation have risen. . . . What was once *religious* belief has now been channeled into *political* belief."[5] Writing of his own Evangelical tradition, Tim Alberta remarks with sadness, "Millions of American Christians . . . after a lifetime spent considering their political affiliations in the context of their faith, are now considering their faith affiliations in the context of their politics."[6]

For Latter-day Saints, the proper ordering of our allegiances is crystal clear. By covenant, we pledge our best efforts not to the success of our party or political views but to building up the Church so that it can play its unique role in the world. Among the first lessons that the Lord impressed upon the heart and mind of Joseph Smith in the early days of the Restoration was the story of Enoch's city. They "were of one heart and one mind, and dwelt in righteousness; and there was no poor among them" (Moses 7:18). Creating that type of community in the Church was the chief goal and the most urgent task of the first Latter-day Saints and set the mark for the type of spirituality to which the Lord calls us in the Restoration. It is a spirituality in which a person sees oneself primarily as someone who is looking for ways to help other people, as our leaders have taught. Current Church President Russell M. Nelson describes that spirituality as an approach to life in which "we strive to build bridges of cooperation rather than walls of segregation."[7]

Our baptismal covenant demands that we strive for unity in the community of believers. In fact, that covenant has less to do with our beliefs than with our willingness to put aside our own interests and work for such unity. According to Alma, the most fundamental impulse that animates our baptismal covenant is not our commitment to a theological proposition (as important as that may be), but the desire "to bear one another's burdens, that they may be light; . . . to mourn with those that mourn . . . and comfort those that stand in need of comfort" (Mosiah 18:8–9) Each week, as we remember that covenant during the sacrament of the Lord's Supper, we are taught yet again that the life of a disciple is inextricably intertwined with the life of her fellow believers. We do not take the sacrament alone. It is an act of communal worship, which means that much more is at work than introspection about our relationship with the Divine. We receive the emblems of Christ's suffering, death, and Resurrection not from an official but from the person who happens to be sitting next to us in the pew. In turn, we offer those emblems to the person on the other side of us. In such a way, we are taught that our primary responsibility within the Church is to give and receive at-one-ment to and from others. We thwart the binding power of this ordinance when we allow something as fleeting as our partisan commitments to prevent us from receiving and giving the at-one-ment it represents.

Rob Daines, president of the Menlo Park California Stake, shared with me this vision of what unity in the Church looks like and the source of its inspiration: "Our favorite stories of Jesus show His love for people on the bottom of the status ladder, the edge of the group, the fringe, the sidelines. You show me your favorite story of Jesus and I'll show you God, through Jesus, reaching out in love to the vulnerable, wounded or ignored. That's what Christ's life is—creating at-one-ment—the love of God and the love of His children. To work in this Church is to stand in the river of God's love for His children. And as I've served in callings in this Church and tried to help His children, I've felt His love for others, and some of that has splashed on me. This Church is a work party, people with picks and shovels trying to help clear the channel for the river of God's love to reach His children at the end of the row. Single, married, gay, straight, Black or white or brown, educated or not, monied or not, employed or not, every race, every class, every person, every political party, mentally or physically ill, there is room for you in this Church. Grab a pick and shovel and join the team."

We must not let our political allegiances get in the way of our more important commitment to help the Church become an instrument for healing and reconciliation in the world. As President Dallin H. Oaks has forcefully directed, "We encourage our members to refrain from judging one another in political matters. We should never assert that a faithful Latter-day Saint cannot belong to a political party or vote for a particular candidate."[8] And if our political allegiances get in the way of that commitment, if they become a source of division within the Church, our regular participation in the sacrament of the Lord's Supper is a recurring reminder that we have pledged to put aside our political preferences for the sake of unity in the Church.

I am a native Washingtonian and have spent much of my life and work involved in the partisan debates that are the air we breathe in the nation's capital. And yet, I have never thought that my views on how best to create a just society are the Lord's. They are mine, and therefore I may be mistaken. I don't think I'm wrong, but I try to be ever mindful of the fact that I might be. Justice Antonin Scalia liked to quote the Puritan revolutionary Oliver Cromwell on this point: "I beseech ye in the bowels of Christ," implored Cromwell, "think that ye might be mistaken." To be sure, the Lord has given us principles to guide us in our efforts at building the City of Man, chief among them being to create a society in which those on the margins can flourish. But how to achieve this objective is a matter about which reasonable patriots can differ. In fact, it is through the exchange of those competing ideas that we make progress as a people.

Latter-day Saints have a sense that we have a special stewardship with regards to preserving the vitality of the Constitution against those whose words and actions serve to weaken the structure of government it creates and the rights it protects. We will honor that stewardship best not by exacerbating the polarization that now defines public life in America—parroting the talking points of the "conflict entrepreneurs"[9] that dominate social media, cable TV, and talk radio—but by drawing upon our experience at building community in our wards and stakes and becoming agents of reconciliation in an increasingly polarized nation.

Within the Nation

The followers of Jesus are called to be "the salt of the earth" (Matthew 5:13), which in part means that we are not to withdraw from society, and therefore we must engage in the hard work of politics. But when we engage in politics, we should do so with a style of our own, and not mimic those who profit from the "outrage industrial complex." President Dallin H. Oaks has described the manner in which Latter-day Saints should engage in politics. He has called for Latter-day Saints to "exercise our influence civilly and peacefully."[10] This is not a new theme. As long ago as 1845, the Twelve Apostles proclaimed to the world the mission of the Latter-day Saints: "To renovate the world—to enlighten the nations—to cover the earth with . . . *union*, peace, and love."[11]

Latter-day Saints have a special responsibility to work as agents of reconciliation and not fan the flames of political division. The Book of Mormon teaches this. As Mormon began his own account on the large plates, he started with the story of how King Benjamin worked his entire life to bring unity to a city divided by class, language, and ethnicity. Surely it is significant that Mormon, who had insight into the unique challenges of our day, began his writings with the story of a person who labored to bring unity to a divided people. And in the apex of the Book of Mormon narrative, the visit of the risen Lord inspires a two-hundred-year period in which there was no contention and no racial, social, or economic divides among the people.

In his book *Bonds of Affection: Civic Charity and the Making of America—Winthrop, Jefferson, and Lincoln*, Elder Matthew S. Holland explains that the idea of "civic charity" was central to the creation of the United States and is indispensable to the success of the Constitution. Embedded in America's DNA from the days of the Massachusetts Bay Colony, perhaps the most eloquent expression of "civic charity" is found in Abraham Lincoln's first inaugural address, delivered during the nation's most perilous moment: "We are not enemies," Lincoln insisted, "but friends. We must not be enemies. Though passion may have strained it must not break our bonds of affection." Lincoln invoked those bonds of affection yet again in his second inaugural address, delivered near the end of a calamitous Civil War that had rendered the Union asunder: "With malice toward none; with charity for all," he implored, "let us strive to . . . bind up the nation's wounds."

Too often those who practice politics play upon passions and biases of the people and use personal attacks against their opponents rather than treating them with respect. Such tactics tear at the social fabric of the nation and undermine the Constitution. As Michael Gerson observed, "The heroes of America are *heroes of unity*. Our political system is designed for vigorous disagreement. It is not designed for irreconcilable contempt. Such contempt loosens the ties of citizenship and undermines the idea of patriotism."[12]

The "civic charity" Holland describes and Gerson demands is the heart and soul of the Constitution of the United States. Surely it is significant that the original Constitution of 1787 was created by compromise among people with deeply held and differing views. Its most important innovation was to establish structures of governance that compel consensus where possible and accommodation where not. To support and defend the Constitution requires more than understanding its various provisions. As important as they are, the First Amendment's guarantee of the "free exercise of religion," the Second Amendment's right to "bear arms," and the Fourteenth Amendment's promise of "equal protection of the laws" are only parts of a much grander governmental design. That design requires compromise. Those who aren't willing to compromise, who aren't willing to settle for less than they would wish so that others may achieve some of what they want, are working at cross-purposes with the Constitution. To support and defend the Constitution, which was created to "establish a more perfect union," requires an unwavering commitment to work for reconciliation and against division.

President Oaks has created a metric for how a follower of Christ should participate in public life: "On contested issues, we should seek to moderate and unify."[13] That prophetically declared standard for our involvement in the public life of the nation challenges all of us. On the contentious issues of the day, those that should be debated vigorously, do we "seek to moderate and unify"? If not, we must change.

President Oaks's challenge sparked a good deal of commentary, and much of what I read and heard involved people on the left and people on the right criticizing each other for not giving heed to his counsel. Their assumption was that he was calling upon others to change, but not them. Several weeks after President Oaks issued his challenge, I attended a Sunday School class that was discussing his remarks. Trying to avoid the finger-pointing that had been all too common in the weeks following President Oaks's remarks, the teacher began the class with this question: "What in President Oaks's talk has caused you to change your approach to contentious public issues?" The first response set the tone for a wonderful discussion. A class member volunteered that he was an active blogger on contentious political matters, and that President Oaks's remarks made him realize that too many of his comments had created further division and were not intended to work for unity. Going forward, he would change his tone. Looking backward, he would reach out to those he had criticized harshly and ask forgiveness. If we are looking for an example of how we can best support and defend the Constitution, we have found it in this brother.

I grew up in the suburbs of Washington, DC, and at a young age developed a deep interest in American politics. Politics were a part of the air we breathed and the water we drank in the nation's capital. I remember watching President Kennedy throw out the first pitch on Opening Day in 1962. I stood along Constitution Avenue with my family and watched his funeral cortege a year later. I lived a short distance from the home of Robert F. Kennedy, whose eleven children were everywhere in our town. I went to school and played sports with the children of congressmen, senators, cabinet secretaries, presidential aides, and Supreme Court justices. I worked on Capitol Hill during summers in high school. There was nothing unusual about any of this. Many of my peers did the same.

During my high school years, my family moved across town

into a new subdivision. We soon discovered that we lived near Mo Udall, who was then a Democratic congressman from Arizona and one of the rising stars on the national political scene. Mo took me under his wing and became a mentor. Although what would become my adult political views differed sharply from his, Udall's kindness to me, his love of country, and his decency to all have inspired me all my life.

I'm not willing to declare that politics are not important. They are. How we go about trying to create a just society under the Constitution is one of the grandest projects in which we can engage. But if our partisan allegiance keeps us from seeing, as Lincoln urged us to see, that our opponents are not enemies, but friends in a common enterprise, we have missed the point of the Constitution, which is to create "a more perfect *union*."

Discussion Questions and Personal Application

1. In what ways can I follow President Oaks's counsel and seek to moderate my views on contested issues for the sake of unity?
2. Do my criticisms of the views of another person avoid calling into question that person's goodness? Do I remind myself that those are the views of a child of God who deserves to be treated with dignity and respect even though I think those views are mistaken?
3. Before criticizing the views of another person, am I certain that I fully understand what the person is saying? Before responding to the argument, can I first restate the argument in my own words to the person's satisfaction?
4. Do I make an effort to gain information from sources that don't share my worldview? Will I read from publications and

listen to voices from the other side of the political spectrum? Am I willing to get my information from sources other than cable news and social media?
5. What is my most important commitment, my chief allegiance? Is it to advance the aims of the political party I favor or to help create unity in God's kingdom?
6. Will I share meals with people whose views on politics are different from my own, and will I listen with respect to their explanations for why they have the views they hold?

Ward Choirs: A Unity Metaphor

KATHY K. CLAYTON

KATHY KIPP CLAYTON spread the gospel worldwide with her husband, Whitney, for nineteen years. She is the mother of seven and the grandmother of thirty-one and the author of *Teaching to Build Faith and Faithfulness* and *Confidence: Your Birthright as a Child of God*.

When our ward choir resumed rehearsing and performing together after a long COVID hiatus, I sang hallelujah—but not because it was written in the music. The ordinances of our sacrament service are not dependent on a ward choir. We don't need a ward choir because there are no other qualified ward members to offer special musical numbers. And we certainly don't turn to a ward choir because the music provided by that amateur group of musicians provides the congregants with music of consistent high quality without a single missed note or cue. I sang hallelujah for the return, at least partly, because all those things are *not* true. Our ward choir, like countless others around the world, is comprised of music-loving amateurs who all live within the same geographic boundaries. We are normal people of all ages, showing up without having been called or even asked personally to do so, simply because of our affection for music and each other. Some of our choir members sing well; some used to sing pretty well but have gotten a little warbly; some have not yet found their voices. All are welcome.

Sometimes we have a true soloist among us. She may technically sing too loudly for a choir performance, but her contribution is just right. Other times we have someone who simply can't seem to hear or duplicate the note as it is written on the printed page. His contribution is just right, too. They all belong. The importance of the excellence of the performance in a traditional sense is trumped by a commitment to each other and to a sound that advances the cause of communal worship. The essential goal is pleasing God and worshiping Him.

Choosing to stay an extra hour on Sundays to rehearse with an amateur ward choir is a choice to opt into a very voluntary association. That choice has long been characteristic of and formative in healthy American society. Perhaps such voluntary association at local levels offers an accessible way forward to fixing local problems of disunity and discord in a down-home way. The choice to associate with others in the neighborhood doesn't need to be via printed music, but it does need to be harmonious and congenial. We don't need to expect government officials or legislation to solve the problem of disunity. Local action—like singing together—can advance the cause of harmony. Choosing to sit side by side and seeking to make acceptable music together can serve as a provocative metaphor of the goal of achieving greater communal unity.

In our homes, families, and communities, we all crave unity, but unity needn't be equated with unison. Determined, ambitious choirs typically choose to sing harmonies more than depending on constant unison. It is easier for groups to sing a single same note than to achieve rich and beautiful harmonies, but the effort required to learn and produce complex musical chords is a worthy one. The resulting music is more interesting, more challenging, and more satisfying.

Similarly, communication that allows for and embraces assorted voices that work thoughtfully together is more interesting, more challenging, and more satisfying.

Choral music offers alternative parts to be hospitable for varying vocal ranges. Choir members sing the notes that are most comfortable for their personal vocal range. Similarly, a generous welcome of diverse points of view is more respectful of preferences and inclinations. A score that welcomes alternative voices embraces a more generous exercise of agency and acknowledgment of personal preferences. Singers don't need to all sing the same note to make beautiful music together.

My husband comes from a family of four boys who all love to sing. A favorite family pastime of theirs is playing their guitars and singing harmonies together. Because there was no sister for their boy band, for decades, the second brother assumed the melody lines and all the high notes. He was good at that and embraced his prominent place in the music-making with aplomb. My husband is the oldest of the four, so it was logical that I would be the first girlfriend to be brought home to join the family fun. I also love to sing, and I quickly assumed what seemed to me to be my obvious claim to the melody lines and the high notes.

It became immediately clear to me that the brother who had long sung those notes had never anticipated a competitor invading his space. Their four-part harmony meant one note per person. I was an intruding number five. We jockeyed for position for a while before I concluded that he wasn't going to relinquish those notes. I considered simply sitting silently, but I knew I would miss being a more robust member of the music-making, so I was determined to find another way forward. I stretched upward to notes above the melody—a descant. A new voice. That second brother smiled at me approvingly. I had successfully found a way to participate without competing. I didn't need to sing more loudly or demand my "rightful" place. With some imagination and respect for and from us all, there was room for every voice, and the music was better because of it. That brother and I still bump into each other occasionally when we sing, but we are both committed to making space for each other. The result is satisfying and sometimes even beautiful.

Historically, people were commonly bound together and unified by blood, geography, religion, and often enemies. Later, democracies were more commonly bound together by social networks with high levels of trust, strong institutions like clubs and churches, and shared stories, like historical heroes and tales of triumph. Today, seeking and creating occasions to sing together in harmony, figuratively speaking, can bind us to each other. Sometimes our "singing" today is cacophonous and performance-oriented instead of cooperative and communal. Everyone seeks to sing louder than everyone else, or to be a soloist. But the music that binds is less performance-based and more cooperative—not necessarily one single, same note, but by decision, harmonious and respectful. To achieve unity, we would spend less time seeking the whole spotlight and more time connecting.

Exemplary choral singers are good listeners. They have a good ear. They are committed to assuring that their voices don't trump the voices seated around them. A choral vocalist who can only hear his own voice and not the ones on either side of him is simply singing too loudly. Careful listening is an essential characteristic of a good choir member. Some quip that we have two ears and one mouth as an indication that we should listen twice as much as we speak. That is good advice.

A friend of mine tells the story of her visit to a grocery store in Texas with her mother. As the two of them stood in the checkout line waiting to pay for their groceries, they uncomfortably overheard the comments of the grumpy woman ahead of them interacting noisily with the cashier. My friend admits that she flippantly whispered to her mother, "Too bad that woman didn't find some personality on aisle 3 and buy it!" Without missing a beat, her mother stepped forward and gently put her hand on the grumpy woman's shoulder, then said in a genuinely solicitous voice, "Are you having a bad day, precious?" The previously grumpy woman burst into tears and launched into a grateful download of her terrible woes. Those two women became fast and enduring friends right there in the checkout line. The cause of unity is advanced when we engage with each other with a spirit of curiosity and care more than one of judgment and criticism. More caring questions, followed by more listening, foster more unity.

I think it must have been terribly frustrating and divisive to have lived in Babel after the Lord had confounded the language of the people. The inability of those people to communicate with one another must have caused enormous discord and confusion. Perhaps today we are suffering from a similar malady—an inability to listen to, value, and understand each other. But God has not done the confounding. We have done it to ourselves. We cut ourselves off from each other when we decline to sing side by side in metaphorical ward choirs. We invite disharmony when we refuse to allow others to make music with us as they sing the notes that work for them. We experience frustration and discord when we cease to be willing to seek new harmonies and to listen to other voices to achieve a pleasing balance. We miss an opportunity to sing hallelujah if we opt out of the unity that comes from making beautiful, comprehensive music together. Long live ward choirs!

Discussion Questions and Personal Application

1. How is "unity" different from "unison"?
2. How can we share our voices in unifying, harmonious ways when others' "notes" or opinions are different from ours? What promotes harmony? What creates dissonance or disharmony?
3. When someone is, figuratively speaking, singing too loudly and disrupting the pleasure and quality of the "music-making," what can another member of the group appropriately and graciously do to positively affect the sound of the song? Might there be occasions when embracing the unilateral volume without comment or intervention would be the higher good?
4. What are organized ways we can choose to associate with people outside our normal spheres of association? How can intentional association in various groups provide us occasion to share our voices in harmonious ways in our modern moment?
5. What do listening and truly hearing have to do with speaking with understanding, grace, and goodness? How can we be more effective listeners?
6. We used to say in our family, "They're both good; they're just different." That reminder served as a dependable response to young proclamations that girls were better than boys, or summer was better than winter. It would also be the right response to any suggestion that tenors are better than basses

WARD CHOIRS: A UNITY METAPHOR

or sopranos better than altos. How can we avoid rushing to assign all ideas and behaviors to a hierarchy of superiority or importance?
7. How can we demonstrate respect and authentic appreciation for the voices and opinions of others?
8. How can we appropriately identify circumstances where the loving exercise of judgment is important (see Moroni 7)? What does that appropriate judgment look and feel like?

And Unity Begat Synergy

H. CRAIG PETERSEN

H. CRAIG PETERSEN has a PhD from Stanford University, taught economics at Utah State University, and later served as mayor of Logan, Utah. He has four children and eleven grandchildren and lives in Logan with his wife, Maradee.

The star attraction at the Cluny Museum in Paris is a series of six 500-year-old tapestries known as The Lady and the Unicorn. Each depicts a noble lady flanked by a lion and a white unicorn. The first five tapestries are generally interpreted as depicting the five human senses and the sixth as representing love or understanding.

Because of the vivid colors and intricate design, the set is often considered the *Mona Lisa* of Middle-Ages tapestries. A close examination reveals that they are made up of thousands of individual threads, each with a color but conveying no meaningful image on its own. Only when considered in the context of the entire tapestries do the separate threads reveal the beauty of the artwork. As J. R. R. Tolkien observed, "The picture is greater than, and not explained by, the sum of the component threads."

The tapestries are an expression of synergy, which can be

defined as an interaction or cooperation giving rise to a whole that is greater than the simple sum of its parts. Common descriptions are that two heads are greater than one or, mathematically, that 2 + 2 can be more than 4. Examples are two horses that synchronize their efforts while pulling a heavy wagon, or two different drugs being used to fight cancer when neither is effective by itself.

Synergy and God's Plan

With the notable exception of Passover, the ancient Israelites created synergy by adding leaven to their bread. In Matthew 13:33, the kingdom of heaven is likened "unto leaven, which a woman took, and hid in three measures of meal, till the whole was leavened." The symbolism was that, on a macro level, the numbers of righteous Saints may be small, but their impact will be magnified as the kingdom of God unfolds to cover the earth.

Synergy is also fundamental to God's plan at the individual level. The Bible Dictionary definition of grace identifies an aspect of grace, in addition to resurrection and cleansing, that is less frequently considered. Through grace, men and women "receive strength and assistance to do good works that they would not be able to maintain if left to their own means." This synergistic boost not only allows us to "overcome" the daily challenges of life; it also gives us the capacity to "become" and to realize our divine potential as literal sons and daughters of God by becoming like our heavenly parents. The enabling aspect of grace is so important that Elder David A. Bednar noted that whenever he encounters the term "grace" in his scripture study, he mentally substitutes "enabling power."[1]

The enabling power associated with grace is a manifestation

of divine power derived from the Atonement of Jesus Christ. It represents God's direct impact on the lives of His children and can take many forms. A powerful example is found in Mosiah. Alma and his people had escaped King Noah only to be captured and put in bondage by Amulon, one of Noah's exiled, wicked priests, who subjected them to physical and emotional abuse. After petitioning God for help, they were enabled: "And now it came to pass that the burdens which were laid upon Alma and his brethren were made light; yea, the Lord did strengthen them that they could bear up their burdens with ease, and they did submit cheerfully and with patience to all the will of the Lord" (Mosiah 24:15). The key to this experience is that the actual nature of their burdens remained unchanged, but they were enabled to "bear them with ease" because they were enabled by God. Another example is "slow of speech" Enoch, who was enabled such that when he spoke, "the earth trembled, and the mountains fled, . . . so great was the power of the language which God had given him" (Moses 6:31; 7:13).

Another source of that enabling power emanates from the interactions of the Saints with each other. An alliterative label is the "synergy of the Saints." There is, or at least can be, a powerful enabling among the members of the Church as they serve and fellowship together. Whatever its members are individually, a ward or branch working and worshiping together becomes more than the sum of its constituent parts. Each person has special needs to be met and unique talents to contribute. As members share one another's burdens, they drink from a collective well of living water that can nourish and sustain everyone.

The influence of the synergy of the Saints is directly related to the unity of the congregation. The scriptures are replete with exhortations to unity. Paul writes, "Now I beseech you, brethren, by the name of our Lord Jesus Christ, that ye all speak the same thing, and that there be no divisions among you; but that ye be perfectly joined together in the same mind and in the same judgment" (1 Corinthians 1:10). Lehi counseled his sons that they should "be men, and be determined in one mind and in one heart, united in all things" (2 Nephi 1:21). The ultimate example is the city of Enoch, which the Lord called Zion, "because they were of one heart and one mind" (Moses 7:18).

Sometimes, unity is mistakenly equated with uniformity, and oneness is taken to mean sameness. To be unified doesn't imply that Church members should be homogenized automatons. Paul understood the distinction in writing to the Church in Rome: "For just as each of us has one body with many members, and these members do not all have the same function, so in Christ we, though many, form one body, and each member belongs to all the others" (Romans 12:4–5, NIV).

President James E. Faust echoed a similar thought: "Within our spiritual unity there is wide room for everyone's individuality and expression. . . . We do not lose our identity in becoming members of this church. We become heirs to the kingdom of God, having joined the body of Christ and spiritually set aside some of our personal differences to unite in a greater spiritual cause."[2]

Elder Dieter F. Uchtdorf taught that unity requires a mighty change of heart. "But that doesn't mean that I'll change my heart to match yours," he explained. "Nor does it mean changing your heart to match mine. Rather, it means changing our hearts to conform with the Savior. . . . The unity we seek is not all standing in the same place, but all looking in the same direction—to Jesus Christ and His glory."[3]

Sources of the Synergy of the Saints

The divine aspect of enabling through grace is not fully understood, but the continual sources of synergy among Church members are more easily identified. Following is a non-exhaustive but useful list.

Specialization of Labor: Productivity in an economic system is enhanced by individuals specializing in tasks for which they are best suited. My personal experience suggests that college professors may not be well suited to toil in wheat fields or to repair cars. The Church is organized in a similar way. Paul wrote that "he gave some, apostles; and some, prophets; and some, evangelists; and some, pastors and teachers" (Ephesians 4:11). Although members of a ward may be asked to serve in many ways over the course of their lives, there is a tendency for those with family history, clerical, teaching, and musical skills to concentrate their time in their areas of special expertise. Being a financial clerk or a choir director can sometimes be a lifetime calling.

This pigeonholing is sometimes welcome and sometimes monotonous to the talented member, but it is often highly beneficial to the other members of the congregation because of the enhanced contributions of skilled practitioners. A professional-quality musical number can be the highlight of a sacrament meeting. Years ago, a priesthood leader called me NOT to be in the ward choir. Many Saints have been unknowingly blessed because I have remained obedient to that bishop's wise counsel.

Role Models: When asked how he achieved so much in math and physics, Isaac Newton replied, "If I have seen further, it is by standing on the shoulders of giants." A careful study of the history of science suggests that few great ideas appear out of nowhere. Rather, they represent the culmination of a series of contributions by many scientists. Similarly, as they progress through their Church experiences, Church members are often benefited by role models at the ward, stake, and general level. Young testimonies are strengthened by the faithfulness and love of Young Women and priesthood leaders. In some cases, a great Church leader may be the only meaningful role model in the life of a young man or woman. Such examples can transcend generations. Thousands of young people have been inspired to be better and do more by ninety-eight-year-old Russell M. Nelson.

Laboratory: A member's ward can be a laboratory for skill and talent development that has spin-offs in the broader arena of life. Youth learn speaking and musical skills. Adults may have their initial leadership opportunities as full-time missionaries or through serving in ward leadership positions. At a relatively young age, I was called as a married student ward bishop and, soon after, as a counselor in the presidency of my resident stake. Those experiences were transformative in helping me survive and navigate through leadership responsibilities in my profession and in local government. Learning to lead in a (usually) supportive Church environment gave me invaluable confidence and experience that was applicable to more confrontational responsibilities.

Emotional Support: Fragile or overwhelmed psyches may be incapable of surmounting the vicissitudes of life. But that which individuals might not be able to overcome alone, they may be able to survive with the help of other Church members. Alma asked that if "ye are desirous to come into the fold of God, . . . and are willing to bear one another's burdens, . . . and are willing to mourn with those that mourn; yea, and comfort those that stand in need of comfort, . . . what have you against being baptized in the name of the Lord?" (Mosiah 18:8–10). Sometimes, there are windows of opportunity that can be opened to save a floundering soul.

As a young bishop, I was sitting on the stand just prior to sacrament meeting when I watched Greg, a young husband, walk out the meetinghouse door. I felt impressed to leave the ninety and nine and go after the one. His church experience that day had not been positive, and he decided he was walking out the door with no intention of ever returning. A little love and a meaningful calling convinced him to give the Church another chance. Greg remains a stalwart member to this day. The essence of this type of synergy is captured by the poet who penned, "I lift thee, and thee lift me, and together we ascend."

Refuge: On the big island of Hawaii, on the Kona Coast, there is a beautiful black sand beach. Today, it has become a tourist attraction, but long before the deluge of tourists, it was known to the Hawaiian people as the City of Refuge. Those who had committed crimes and were being sought after for punishment could escape consequences for their actions if they could reach the black sands of the "city." There, they were guaranteed protection. A local congregation can serve a similar function. The members may not be fugitive criminals, but we are all sinners seeking sanctuary of some kind. Hopefully, as the hymn "Sweet Is the Peace the Gospel Brings" suggests, Church involvement will provide refuge from tensions at home or at work. In particular, temples are the Lord's City of Refuge from the cares of the world.

Joint Understanding and Commitment to a Common Purpose: Political views may be divergent. Individual tastes and preferences are, by definition, highly varied. Although there may be some differences in how members interpret certain gospel principles and policies, we all have the ultimate goal of returning to live with our heavenly parents and experiencing eternal happiness. That common focus creates what might be considered as a "gospel shorthand" that doesn't have to be repeatedly voiced or established, but is implicitly understood by the Saints.

Synergy Lost?

In today's increasingly polarized society, it may be more difficult to maintain spiritual unity while allowing for individuality and expression. To the extent that these values are inappropriately entangled, the enabling, synergistic impact of Church involvement is muted because, as the title of this essay states, "unity begat synergy."

Joint understanding may be increasing over time as instructional efforts improve and information about Church history is more available and candid. However, at least one aspect of common purpose seems to be a casualty of today's world. When the Saints were building the Nauvoo Temple during the 1830s, it was a joint effort of members bringing their varied skills and equipment to the task. The project focused their time and talents on a common, unifying goal.

Church work projects continued into the twentieth century in the form of chapel building and Church farm activities. Such opportunities haven't entirely disappeared, but they are much less common than in the past. As a result, with the notable exception of the many hours that Church leaders and others spend in individual service each week, we have become more of a Sunday church.

But even Sunday church has changed. The two-hour block has diminished the time members spend interacting with each other on Sunday. Relief Societies and elders quorums gather less frequently, and there is one fewer break time between meetings that enables members to socialize and become better acquainted. At my stage in life (retired), I crave more interactions, but find my Sunday church experience to be less socially satisfying than it used to be. Although my primary reason for going to church is to worship, positive experiences with other good people during my meeting block have always been important to me. Now, it's more like ships passing in the night. My wife says I should grumble less and be more proactive. She's right. But still.

COVID-19 restrictions have also had a significant impact. Some have found that worshiping from home seems to be a perfectly acceptable alternative. Will Zoom and podcasts become the new once-a-week Rameumptom that enables people to disengage from traditional joint worship with its synergistic benefits? If the synergy of the Saints is eroding, is that loss an episodic phenomenon caused by unique circumstances (the pandemic and unusually deep political divisions), or is it a long-term trend associated with more individualized worship and an increasingly secular society?

Assuming that divisiveness today is more pronounced and that the trend will continue, why? One explanation as to why Church members in particular and Americans in general are so divided is that we no longer have common sources of information that serve as a baseline for secular discussion; we no longer accept the same truth. The agreed-upon starting point for dialogue has been eroded. In contrast, for gospel principles there is a widely accepted core—the scriptures and the teachings of the living prophets.

I am continually amazed by how many people get all of their current-event news from a small number of sources that make no pretense of objectivity. Some cable news channels quickly come to mind, but at least they have some minimal reputation to uphold. But the conspiracy theorists that troll the internet are unconstrained. Much of today's dialogue is a little like trying to do math with no agreement as to whether we should use base 10 or base 2, or maybe like discussing geography without starting from the premise that the earth is round.

The greater difficulty in having robust, stimulating political discussions without rancor, even with some Church members, leaves me feeling even more isolated. I have to conceal a part of me for the sake of social harmony. With some of my family and friends there is an unspoken agreement that to preserve harmonious relationships, the discussion of certain topics is taboo. Understood. But how much time can we spend looking at pictures of grandchildren and recounting our last medical procedure?

Conclusion

Years ago, I knew a special family with three boys rather close in age. They lived on a farm, and the whole family gathered for an early supper each day. During the meal they would aggressively debate the issues of the day or deep philosophical concepts. Each young man was bright and opinionated, and the discussions often became heated and loud. But when the meal was finished, the debate abruptly ended and they jointly returned to their labors in the fields as a unified team. The unspoken premise was that unity in the family trumped everything else because family came first. That mentality needs to exist in Church congregations.

For the synergy of the Saints to have maximum effect, members need to participate in Church activities with the perspective that testimony-building and gospel understanding should overshadow politics and personalities. Newton stood on the shoulders of giants. We would do well to avoid standing on the toes of others.

Discussion Questions and Personal Application

1. How have you seen the "synergy of the Saints" eroding, if it is? Is that erosion temporary, caused by unique circumstances of our time, or is it a long-term trend associated with more individualized worship and an increasingly secular society?
2. How comfortable do you feel expressing different ideas or points of view in priesthood or Relief Society meetings? How can you contribute to building an environment where others express their points of view?
3. What skills or traits have you learned or refined through Church service that have had a major impact in other aspects of your life?
4. Who were your Church role models who significantly impacted your life? Were any of them unlikely role models because they were different from you?
5. Are we becoming "Rameumptom" Church members? How can you feel more connected to your ward or branch now?
6. How often do you find it necessary to conceal your opinions for the sake of harmony? In family gatherings? At social events? In church? How do you handle differences of opinion?

The Gardener King

ADAM TIMOTHY

ADAM TIMOTHY holds an MBA from Oxford University and runs an aerospace firm on the East Coast. He and his wife, Eva, are parents to three and reside in Newbury, Massachusetts.

As I write this essay, it is spring, the gardening has begun, and I've just read about King Benjamin getting his hands dirty to feed himself. This concept of a Gardener King, one willing to assume great responsibility without overindulging in the privileges of power, is all too rare in history. Although, Christ certainly is its ultimate archetype, and it is intriguing that Mary mistook the risen Lord for just such.

In the midst of attempts to prepare the New England soil, this past weekend was general conference, and a number of points were made in seeking to address the growing contention and division both within the Church and the world at large.

Currents of contemporary culture notwithstanding, it seemed clear that God's kingdom revolves less around activism—hoping that God will rally around our viewpoint—than it does around acting in faith, even when we can't see or understand the full picture at present.

With the garden in mind and the division at hand, the allegory of the vineyard related by Jacob in the Book of Mormon seems particularly apt.

The first problem that arises is that of the roots and branches vying for prominence. This sort of contention is familiar to many, as it runs the gamut from political ideologies, to the generation gap in families, to the individual seeking to find proper balance and perspective.

Here the roots represent history, tradition, that which has been proven in the laboratory of time—and looking back to the foundations upon which we build lives and society.

The branches, in their turn, are the visions and dreams, the expansion and exploration into that which is not yet known, the reaching out toward the unfamiliar and marginalized and the light of what is possible.

Both are meant to broaden in their sphere, and both contribute greatly to the welfare of the tree. Indeed, plant biology and photosynthesis require that both work in harmony, xylem and phloem, to maintain a balance wherein each feeds and nourishes the other.

Yet, as this allegory illustrates, it is the nature of each to lose perspective of the tree in its effort to strengthen and establish its own position as superior. It can be hard for either the earth-mover or the star-seeker to turn around and see what it is that they are ultimately trying to create. Drawing strength to itself, stubborn dogmatism and enlightened despotism are both examples of a type of loftiness that throws the system out of whack and makes bitter its fruits.

Alongside this arboreal balancing act, there is something else at play. An effort by the gardener to spur His vineyard to fruitfulness through grafting.

In this mixing of cultures, ideas, and backgrounds we find a stirring call to the congregation or community that may have started feeling a bit too settled in.

But doing the work of opening ourselves up to receive, to make room for and to make the outsider feel welcome, is often going to be uncomfortable for both sides at the outset. It requires sincere efforts and may even result in friction at times.

It can all seem like a big ask.

In my own experience, I've found it can be particularly challenging to push my present mindset and perspective toward greater openness. I like to feel like I've "progressed" and that my current perspective is the most accurate one. After all, it represents the learning and experience of all that has come before, so surely my views now must be better informed and more mature than what I knew as a child or a teenager or a young parent.

The problem, though, is that I keep running into experiences where my self-confirmed views feel a lot like Jell-O: well-set through time, but not all that solid a foundation for capturing the broad scope of life. In parenting, for instance, it's easy to assume that whatever pops into my head is in the best interest of my teen children, as I've already had the experience of being in their shoes. But, I've learned that simply living through an experience and actually remembering it deeply to the point where you can listen, understand, and show real empathy are two very different things. In fact, it's often the case that my frustrations with my younger self come through more readily than the compassion I ought to feel in having lived through many of the trials and struggles my children now face.

Over the course of my life, I've spent plenty of time in the figurative branches of the tree as well as among its roots. I'm older, hopefully a bit wiser, and, in theory, after all this experience I should be seeing the whole tree and the big picture more fully. And yet, I still find myself caught up in obstinacy and a narrow perspective at times, particularly when I don't have all the answers I'd like to have.

Considering these challenges, how exactly are we to reach this unifying combination of courage and compassion, energy and openness, conviction and humility?

Well, as it happens, the Gardener King had his sleep disturbed one night by an angel who delivered and provided the answer to this very question.

The power to overcome the allure of power, the capacity to confront our myopic tendencies, the strength to soften our hearts—each of these comes through the Atonement of Jesus Christ, which returns to us the soul of a little child.

If becoming as little children seems like an overly simplistic answer to an incredibly complex web of backgrounds, identities, and ideologies, it may be that this is precisely the point. This might be what Oliver Wendell Holmes Jr. was referring to as "simplicity on the other side of complexity."

A fresh perspective where so many of the complications and nuances that justify division and contention lose their draw because there are too many wonderful, exciting, and unifying discoveries happening to be bothered by them. In a gospel that offers the opportunity of being "born again," we get to jettison the gravity of cynicism in favor of an imagination that encompasses every good thing and that sets our souls soaring as on eagles' wings.

As little children, our focus is on learning, loving, building, growing, and moving forward in life. Forgiveness is offered freely because grudges weigh us down and hold us back. We withhold the aspersions of instantaneous judgment because we are still figuring things out ourselves. We listen because there is wisdom to be found in hearing. Different thoughts, ideas, and even people are considered in ways that stretch the mind and heart and that ultimately expand the vision and souls of all involved.

As little children, we don't have to worry about having all the answers right now. We can concentrate our efforts instead on growing "in grace and in the knowledge of the truth" (D&C 50:40). In this place of spiritual perspective, we find that we are able to assimilate each ray of light we come across within the incredible foundation of restored truth we are building upon.

And the invitation is to all.

As both adult parents and their adolescent offspring become as little children, they are able to see each other more clearly, relating to their ultimate purpose as individuals and a family unit. And for those standing ready to draw battle lines to defend a favored view, it is often the case that, in lowering our walls, we will all be afforded a better view. A view of the tree in its fullness; a diverse and marvelous network connected by the mediating power of a Savior who has redeemed us all. Freedom, forgiveness, and grace are spread through its every fiber.

And when such are allowed to flow freely, the fruit that follows is truly "most desirable above all things" (1 Nephi 11:22), for it is the love of God; all that any of us came here to find.

For just a moment, unleash your inner child's imagination and consider just how wonderful that fruit tastes to the soul, how very deeply we yearn for it, and lastly, how everyone around us is ultimately seeking this very thing.

Sure, there are plenty of scary things in the world: dark spaces, evil thoughts, and horrific acts at home and abroad. But, as Saints, we are not called upon to give ear to our fears. Ours is the call, rather, to follow in the footsteps of those before us, who spread their light even when the darkness seemed impenetrable. Footsteps like those of the man whose life's work would become the keystone of our religion. One who, when confronted with corruption, betrayal, atrocity, and the loss of so much that he had held dear, still transcribed the words, "I fear not what man can do; for perfect love casteth out all fear. And I am filled with charity, which is everlasting love; wherefore, all children are alike unto me; wherefore, I love little children with a perfect love; and they are all alike and partakers of salvation" (Moroni 8:16–17).

May we each experience this rebirth, this putting off the natural man and donning instead that transfiguring mantle of childlike charity. May we lift our lights as both beacons of welcome and in seeking to illuminate those spaces we do not yet comprehend in full.

And may we eagerly tend to the garden of the Lord, even Zion, that its fruits might be the at-one-ness of a people in whose hearts the love of God has grown to fullness.

Discussion Questions and Personal Application

1. A gardener king might be described as one who exercises his or her power in the selfless acts of nurturing and service. What do King Benjamin's example and words teach us about becoming gardeners for our fellow men and women? (See "Our Earthly Stewardship" by Bishop Gérald Caussé [*Liahona*, November 2022].)
2. We often refer to Christ as the Great Mediator between us and the justice of God. How might that title also apply to our

relationships with one another and the reconciliation of diverse worldviews?
3. How might a graft of outside perspectives benefit the community as a whole? What efforts can we make to help a graft succeed?
4. Christ asks us to take His yoke, not because He is so strong and powerful, but because He is meek and lowly of heart (see Matthew 11:29). Why does meekness play such a central part in our work toward unity?
5. When we are tempted to become defensive or to close down emotionally, in what ways might adopting the perspective of a little child help us in retaining both composure and compassion?

Rocky Ground

KIMBERLY TEITTER

KIMBERLY A. TEITTER, PsyD, is a licensed clinical psychologist and adjunct instructor in the Department of Psychiatry at the University of Utah. At time of writing, she is also serving as a bishop's wife and is mother to two daughters.

I believe it is no accident that the Savior frequently used metaphors about growing and tending the earth to teach us a variety of lessons—about diversity and unity, understanding who we are, what our role is in the body of Christ, how we can tell what will be effective (or fruitful) action, and just how much *work* it will require from us to become the people that He wants us to be. I developed an interest in gardening when I moved from the deep South to Utah, at first being attracted to the benefits of the harvest, but continuing (in spite of a steep learning curve) because of the opportunities it gave me to meditate on spiritual matters. As I reflect on the current state of unity in the Church of Jesus Christ and identify areas for growth, some of these lessons gleaned from the wisdom of the earth readily come to mind as apt for how we can progress together as Saints in the kingdom.

In the parable of the sower, Jesus's first recorded parable in the book of Matthew, He relates: "A farmer went out to sow his seed. As he was scattering the seed, . . . some fell on rocky places, where it did not have much soil. It sprang up quickly, because the soil was shallow. But when the sun came up, the plants were scorched, and they withered because they had no root" (Matthew 13:3–6, NIV).

I reflect on this passage often as I effortfully till the rough and chunky dirt in the backyard of my Utah home we moved into two years ago, accompanied with a sense of wistfulness for the fertile soil of my North Carolina hometown. I had always believed that nothing could grow in rocky soil, so when I saw all of the different kinds of plants that were growing in my yard, I thought that my new home was promising for a new garden. However, I quickly realized that many of those plants were *weeds*. Granted, the term is subjective, but invasive species of all kinds tend to thrive with little nutrients and still manage to develop deep and enduring roots. I frequently think to myself that I could dig to the very core of the earth and still find the watery white roots of the morning glory down there!

When I think about the dynamics in the Church today, one of the things that keeps me anchored to gospel principles is the promise of Zion, a place where all of God's children can be of one heart and mind and dwell in righteousness and equity (see Moses 7:18). There are a number of things that renew my faith that the gospel will flourish—looking at a growing membership of people outside of the United States, the growth of humanitarian efforts, and the development of different partnerships. My heart swelled, for example, when the Church announced its partnership with the NAACP in 2018; as a Black woman, I recognized the decades of healing that had to take place on both sides as two organizations committed to turning toward the Lord and to each other.

On a local level, I have had wonderful experiences in congregations that gathered together people from all different walks of life and successfully brought them together in harmony. I have learned, however, that even though in some areas the gospel truth grows strong, other environments may give the appearance of fertile ground while being rocky underneath—almost "having a form of godliness, but denying the power thereof" (2 Timothy 3:5). Oftentimes a testimony springing forth from this environment values practices over principles and culture over cultivation, which will appear to grow strong until tested by the realities of a challenging and nuanced world.

For example, the Church has many open avenues of communication and pathways of knowledge: we believe in personal revelation, which allows each person to lead his or her stewardship in a Christlike manner; we have a lay ministry system in which any person of almost any age can be a teacher of gospel principles; we have materials printed and produced in dozens of languages and broadcast throughout the world; and we have a proselytizing force of missionaries and ministers to take that message into the world. And yet, with all the access to communication, which would seemingly expand our perspectives, it amazes me how easy it is for the invasive processes of enmity and mutual disregard to grow. Especially in the Church in America, the seeds of mutual understanding and respect seem to be crowded out by the quickly rooting belief that people can be reduced to political talking points or ideologies. Polarizing perspectives on hot topics of the day, such as race, gender, and sexuality, also seem to take root and spread quickly, such that it becomes overwhelming to weed out extremes and sow truth and light. I can remember when many Church members spoke out against the organization Black Lives Matter, claiming that their statement calling to support one another in extended families and "villages" rather than only in nuclear families was against gospel principles. What a strange thing to object to, I thought, from members of a Church who all recognize the reality of an extended family network by calling non-relatives "brothers and sisters"!

There are also those who would use their status as members of the Church as means to exalt themselves or claim a moral high ground, distorting the gospel's truth claims to be exclusionary to others. There are so many people in the world who are not of our faith but are nevertheless not out of the expanse of God's love, nor out of our responsibility to minister. I have experienced the pain of people using their membership in the Church as a means to suppress or oppress views that they are afraid of, or to mask their own flaws and biases.

On my first job in Utah as a clinician on an inpatient unit, I experienced a family who in their distress likely made assumptions about my skill level or ability to relate to their family. I learned later that everything I said was misinterpreted by the client to be malicious, but no feedback was ever provided. On the last day of the patient's stay, when I was moved off of the case without explanation, I reached out to the family to ask for clarification. I surmised that they had felt (unjustly and incorrectly) that I had been judging their family, which was an affront to the work I had done. But most hurtful to me, the client's parent told me that he had consulted with his stake president, who was a higher-level administrator in the system where I worked, and that they planned to pursue disciplinary action. Though further action was never taken, I was fearful for many months after that about the future of my livelihood. I had never so blatantly experienced someone using an identity that was so precious to me as a means to *intimidate* me, with no evidence needed other than inaccurate perception.

The belief that sameness is necessary for unity is another popular prevailing thought that may appear to produce viable fruit, but may also be a weed that has taken root in rocky soil. When I consider the history of the early Saints, I recognize that there were justifiable reasons and perhaps even systemic advantages for keeping a homogenous, tight-knit group as they moved across the plains, to mitigate the danger that came from opposition. However, what may have formerly been a useful strategy has transformed into a pattern of relating to one another that creates in-groups and out-groups. Such a manner of thinking tends to make us dubious of difference, such that anyone who departs from what we are used to thinking of as traditional or "safe" in the Church becomes depicted as an outsider to the faith, despite the level of that individual's devotion.

Early on in my gardening journey, I once had a volunteer plant that I did not recognize, something that took root after being scattered by the wind or other means rather than being planted on purpose. I left it in my garden bed for a while to see if it would grow into a flower or something similarly delightful, but after two weeks and four feet of growing, it had produced only spade-shaped leaves and a slightly spiky and spiny stem. I was worried that if I let it grow, it would take over my planting space, so I started to pull it out. However, when I began the task, I found that the roots were deep and wide-branching, so much so that it was hard to pull. I then decided to chop the stem, but even that was difficult because it was so thick and watery. When I was halfway through my butchering job, I realized that I had probably made a mistake and should have left this plant to grow a little longer. And the next year when I saw those plants growing in another space, I learned to recognize a sunflower when I saw one.

How often do we as members become afraid when people are different from us? How often do we fail to recognize the beauty of someone's spiritual journey because we have not seen something grow that way before? How often do we pull our heavenly siblings out or chop them down before their flower can bloom, declaring their experiences to be too much for us to be willing to support? Ironically, when these Saints leave the fold after not feeling supported, they may even have their experiences disregarded by using them as an analog to the very parable I am expounding. In cultivating the kingdom where all God's children are meant to thrive, we would take care to recognize the gifts of a diverse membership, and not wait until we have made the mistake of cutting them out to mourn what we have lost.

The Savior teaches that seeds planted on rocky soil will eventually wither, which strengthens my faith that God will prevail over these patterns of belief. The responsibility falls to those who would call themselves laborers in the kingdom to prepare for this to happen, and work to free the ground from these weeds that affect the harvest. I have learned that you can in fact grow a number of things in rocky soil, but it requires great amounts of mindful preparation tailored to the desire of the planting space. Experienced gardeners measure the pH balance of the soil, or recognize from the types of plants that are growing successfully what nutrients are likely to be in the ground; they then use this information to alter the balance of those nutrients so that the type of plants they *want* to grow are able to thrive there. They may grow other plants there with the design of loosening the soil or providing complementary "companions" for future seedlings. Without that preparation, it becomes more likely that the seeds planted on rocky soil will wither and die for not being able to take adequate root.

What would it look like to employ this same mindful preparation when trying to help unity take root in the Church today? I believe it would take more than a passive acceptance of the "fruit" that grows from our culture or our practices, but rather a values-guided drive toward building the kingdom of God on earth. When we truly set our focus on love for God and love for one another being the fruit that we want to grow, we might prepare by planting "companions" of acceptance, proximity to difference, kindheartedness, tenderness, and other Christlike qualities that help us as mortals learn how to love more perfectly as Christ did.

President Russell M. Nelson teaches that the most important identity that we have is as children of God,[1] and within that total, all-encompassing community, it seems that being a member of the Church loses some of its peculiarity and becomes more of the norm, such that we can interpret Church membership as a "culture-less" experience where only the culture of Christ prevails. And wouldn't that be a lovely vision!

When Elder Quentin L. Cook first spoke on this idea in 2018, I embraced the idea of a unifying culture of Christ as much as anyone.[2] I loved the vision of creating Zion together by seeing our differences as ancillary to our connection with each other and with God. But I can remember this being depicted on a local level that reducing the *importance* (not the centrality) of other identities is what will bring unity in the kingdom. Among members of the Church who also have marginalized identities in society, the implication is that other identifiers such as race, gender, or sexual orientation are not important. Functionally, I understand that it may comfort some who wish to assuage previous pain points in Church history around such identities by turning our attention to our unifying divine nature, which consequently (as President Nelson has said in recent years) also allows us to access the love that God has for His children. But I have seen members of the Church urge others of our siblings to leave the fold, saying that there is no place for them as long as they turn to identifiers of "the world."

I vividly remember a Relief Society lesson on Quentin L. Cook's talk "Prepare to Meet God," which discussed this idea of the culture of Christ. I shared some of the pain I experienced as a Black woman to feel a sense of belonging and receptiveness to my experiences in Church settings, which did not seem to me to be a reflection of Christlike love. The teacher responded that perhaps I should set aside my identity, stop "feeling" different, and open my heart to reaching out to other people. Thankfully, a sweet sister spoke up and said that she had seen my actions and my efforts to unify the ward, naming a few auspicious examples, and noted that there were very few people she had met that embodied the message of the talk more than me. It was a boon to my soul to feel that one person could see how I strove to honor my identity as a child of God above all else, even while I have different earthly experiences.

While I understand the intent to have the Saints focus on the source of our eternal worth, I acknowledge that it feels like an assumption to make of one who names other identities as being important, to imply that that person believes that they are more *central* than their spiritual identities. In fact, I believe that God *designed* my different lenses to help me access my spiritual gifts and navigate through this world. It is through my experiences as a Black woman that I have developed my empathy for my heavenly siblings, patience with imperfect Church leaders, and faith in a God who is able to direct our paths for good.

During one of my more successful planting years, I decided

to tap into native wisdom on companion planting and try what is referred to as a Three Sisters plot, which is when you grow corn, beans, and squash together. I was skeptical because I had experienced challenges with a successful harvest with all three of those plants individually: corn wanted to be planted in big groups, but grows so tall and heavy that it is prone to falling; beans would shrivel in the heat and tangle on the ground; and squash was the bane of my existence due to a particular type of pest that lays eggs on the back of the leaves, an issue that if not handled quickly will decimate the crop. But miraculously, when grown together, the corn supports the beans and the squash to be able to grow freely, while the winding of the vines also supports the corn on its own trellis. The beans are shaded by the other two plants so that they are able to thrive in the shade while the sun-loving plants soak up the light. I also found very few of the dreaded "squash bugs."

The three plants, with their distinctive issues as individual plants, were able to grow together and reach their full individual potential with the support of the other plants and their unique characteristics. Likewise, I dream of a Zion in which it is not necessary for people to shed the things that make them unique, but accept and dedicate those differences to the building of the kingdom. In recent years, Quentin L. Cook said, "We can be an oasis of unity and celebrate diversity. Unity and diversity are not opposites. We can achieve greater unity as we foster an atmosphere of inclusion and respect for diversity. . . . Our members and new converts often come from diverse racial and cultural backgrounds. . . . Yet we can be united in our love of and faith in Jesus Christ."[3] I love the metaphor of an *oasis* when describing what we as unified Saints can create together when we fully embrace diversity, to envision a lush and fertile spot of growth and development in the midst of a desert of dissension and division. I believe that we all have experiences that could help one another; in fact, it may only be together that we grow to reach the full potential that our heavenly parents have in store for us.

May the God who has not given us the spirit of fear of one another grant us the wisdom to embrace a love that exists not in spite of, but because of, our unique design.

Discussion Questions and Personal Application

1. I used the scriptural passage of seeds planted on rocky soil to describe the challenges I see with respect to having unity within diversity in the Church today. What metaphors, in nature or elsewhere, do you find resonant to describe this issue?
2. What are the conditions you have observed in your spheres of influence that make for a "fertile ground" for unity? What conditions have you observed that provide challenges for unity?
3. How has the polarization of our culture today affected your viewpoint of others? Are you more or less likely to be open to different perspectives as a result? Where do you think it is helpful to be open? Where do you think it is *less* helpful to be open?
4. What do you see as your personal "value drive" to build the kingdom of God on earth? In what ways have you demonstrated action consistent with your values? In what ways can you do more?
5. Think of people in your ward or other spheres of influence that hold different cultural identities than you. How are you conscious of their identity as a child of God? In what ways does their difference add to your understanding that they are children of God?
6. What are some ways we can embrace our central identity as children of God while also fostering an atmosphere of inclusion and respect for diversity?

The UNITY and Strong Families of "Nothingness"

LINDA AND RICHARD EYRE

RICHARD AND LINDA EYRE are *New York Times* #1 bestselling authors who lecture throughout the world on parenting, life balance, and most recently, grandparenting. Linda is a musician (violin) and cofounder of Joy Schools, and Richard holds a Harvard MBA and ran for Utah governor. Former mission leaders in London, they are parents of nine and grandparents of thirty-four. The Eyres live in Park City, Utah.

The Five Ds

It may seem normal and even necessary to have discord, division, dissension, and even a bit of dismissal and disrespect in politics and government, because that is essentially the way democracies function, and the goal is not really unity, but progress through diversity and differences that are debated and compromised and built into coalitions producing laws and policies for the common good. Or, said another way, democratic government works when

THE UNITY AND STRONG FAMILIES OF "NOTHINGNESS"

we are united on the most important goals, but divided on how to get there.

The Church, as a theocracy, works in a very different way, because instead of competing and picking between rival leaders and alternative ideologies or philosophies, we follow one Divine Leader and adhere to His higher laws and doctrine. The very things that can save a democracy, or make it thrive—competition, compromise, and collective polarizing—can undermine and harm the Church.

Man's government is a fluid thing that we strive to make better over time as we try to understand and meet collective needs. God's government is His gospel and His priesthood, and it needs no improvement because it is perfect.

Yet both Church and state evolve and progress—but for very different reasons and in very different ways. Those who believe in progressive democracy would say that civil society grows better and more complete as we learn where and how to improve government and where and how to limit it. Those who believe in an ongoing Restoration would say that our view of the gospel and our participation here in God's kingdom grow fuller and more complete as more of it is continually restored. The former is hastened by taking sides, debate, activism, and even civil disobedience, while the latter is hastened by prayer, forgiveness, long-suffering, and obedience, and by letting God prevail.[1]

Both Church and state, in order to survive and thrive and grow, need all the unity we can discover within them. In government we need a unity of purpose that can be difficult to find in democracies where the people are not united and where "the loyal opposition" is always a necessary component. Theoretically, unity in the gospel should be much easier, as we seek the mind and will of our heavenly parents rather than the compromised will of men.

Family—The Deepest Division

The Five Ds, dangerous but potentially productive in the state, and dangerous and potentially destructive in the Church, become disastrous and potentially spirit-destroying in families.

In a community or a county, they can be stimulating. In a stake or in a ward, they can be painful and undermining. But when they take root in a *family*, they hurt most deeply and can seem to endanger even the very plan of God.

In the Latter-day Saint paradigm, family is not only the basic unit of our society, culture, and economy, but of our *eternity*. Family is the gift of mortality that makes us, potentially, more like our heavenly parents. In his classic, purpose-summarizing couplet, President Russell M. Nelson tells us that the gospel is "home-centered, Church-supported," mirroring the earlier metaphor of President Harold B. Lee, who called the Church the scaffolding with which we build eternal families.[2]

The point is not that we should have expectations of never disagreeing with family members, or that we should beat ourselves up with discouragement when there is contention in our homes—rather, the point is understanding that all of our hopes and efforts and strivings for unity should peak within our immediate and extended families, because it is that family, not the Church, that is potentially eternal—and that can be the direct mirror of our once and future heavenly home—and that is, in fact, the very Government of God.

How

Lovely as the words are, we might also find some dark or ironic humor in some of the lyrics of our beloved hymn "Love

THE UNITY AND STRONG FAMILIES OF "NOTHINGNESS"

at Home." "In the cottage there is joy . . . peace and plenty here abide, smiling sweet on every side . . . time does softly, sweetly glide . . . all the earth's a garden sweet, making life a bliss complete." We are always tempted to change the last line to "when there's no one home."

Families, with their close quarters, different personalities, and interlaced responsibilities and obligations sometimes seem the perfect breeding ground for the Five Ds. Is there any simple solution for a problem as complex and varied as contention and discord in a family? Or is it a complicated, multifaceted monster that can only even be approached by a combination of prayer, therapy, spiritual counseling, and priesthood blessings?

While all of these approaches, and anything else we can think of, are worthy of pursuit in the quest for something as eternally important as familial peace and unity, the premise of this essay is that there actually is *one* single and enormously effective and impactful direction that all of us ought to try to understand and apply. But while it is simple in its premise and concept, it may be the hardest of all forms of God-directed self-improvement. It is something called "nothingness."

Nothingness, and Its Promises

The nothingness contemplated here is what Alma spoke of as non-compelled humility. He preached, "He that truly humbleth himself, and repenteth of his sins, and endureth to the end, the same shall be blessed—yea, much more blessed than they who are compelled to be humble" (Alma 32:15). Perhaps, among other things, he was comparing himself with his own father in a complementary way. Alma the Younger had been humbled in the most compelling way imaginable—by the powerful visit of an angel of the Lord. Alma the Elder had humbled himself based on the words of Abinadi, a prophet from the wilderness who no one else believed.

But the consummate and defining explanation of nothingness comes from King Benjamin, and it is his matchless discourse that connects it to family and to unity in the most profound and significant way. In verse 11 of Mosiah chapter 4, near the midpoint of his speech, Benjamin gives a pointed and singular admonition: "Remember, and always retain in remembrance, the greatness of God, and your own nothingness."

In all of scripture, that may be the most consequence-connected and promise-laden advice ever given. Verses 12–16 connect that single direct admonition to seventeen remarkable promises. It makes the "if-then" connection clearly and directly: *If* ye shall do this (*remember your own nothingness*), ye *shall* or ye *will* . . . The proffered promises are comprehensive:

"always rejoice"
"be filled with the love of God"
"always retain a remission of your sins"
"grow in the knowledge of the glory of him that created you"
"[grow] in the knowledge of that which is just and true"
"not have a mind to injure one another"
"live peaceably"
"render to every man according to that which is his due"
"not suffer your children that they go hungry, or naked"
"[not] suffer that [your children] transgress the laws of God"
"[nor] fight and quarrel one with another"
"[nor] serve the devil"
"teach [your children] to walk in the ways of truth and soberness"

THE UNITY AND STRONG FAMILIES OF "NOTHINGNESS"

"teach them to love one another"

"[teach them] to serve one another"

"succor those that stand in need of your succor"

"not suffer that the beggar putteth up his petition to you in vain"

What would you give to have that list of promises? King Benjamin tells us we must give just one thing—a form of non-compelled humility that is so deep that he calls it "nothingness."

A careful pondering of the seventeen promises suggests that they are all about peace and love and family and unity—the kind of unity that we cannot earn, and that can be given only by the Spirit of God, the kind that is invited and petitioned for through a paradigm of nothingness.

Indeed, all of the Five Ds, and the enmity that can stem from them, begin with pride. They flourish when we fight to prove we are right and forget that it is He who is right; they spark and grate and irritate and react when our hearts are tuned to our egos, our needs, our glory, and they dissipate and harmonize when those hearts turn to His love and His glory.

In that heart-turning process, and in the presence of His Spirit that shines into and through our nothingness, each of the seventeen promises is a natural, even logical outgrowth or consequence. They all happen because of the clarity and charity of who we are within our prayed-for and accepted and non-compelled humility.

Long before we have attained it, we can begin to imagine ourselves in that perspective of nothingness and in that awareness of God's "everythingness" and begin to feel how each of those seventeen promises can flow from this replacement of pride with humility. And that lovely bit of imagination may be enough to start us on the long and hard pursuit of the actual quality.

This may be the *flow* of which the Lord speaks in Doctrine and Covenants 121 after His admonishments of the patient and long-suffering ways that the priesthood is rightfully and peacefully used (another if-then connection): "The Holy Ghost shall be thy constant companion, . . . and without compulsory means it shall flow unto thee forever and ever" (v. 46).

In Families

In the frantic, self-absorbed world we live in, keeping and holding to this paradigm of humility and nothingness in our families is not always easy, no matter how much we believe it. We can think of so many falling-short examples in our own family. And they have gone on for so many years.

One of the earliest that comes to my mind (Richard) happened in the middle of one night during our Washington, DC, years. Our first little baby, Saren, slept in the next room, and my problem (here we go with the "my") was that I'm a lighter sleeper than Linda, so whenever Saren woke up, I woke up, and as always there were three potential courses of action: 1. Pretend to be asleep and hope Linda would wake up soon and deal with it, 2. Nudge Linda a little to help her wake up and deal with it, or 3. Do the right thing and get up quick before the crying awoke Linda.

That night I did number 3, but was soon regretting it. I actually had a meeting the next morning at the White House, and I needed a good night's sleep (here we go with the "I"). I took Saren in the kitchen out of Linda's earshot, but nothing I could think of to do would calm her down—the diaper, the bottle, the blankie—nothing helped. An hour went by—only walking around holding her helped. Then another hour. I was angry (not at her, I told myself, at the *situation*).

THE UNITY AND STRONG FAMILIES OF "NOTHINGNESS"

I kept pacing, and finally grace came in the form of a little epiphany. The moon was shining that night, and as I stared at Saren's little sniffling moonlit face, it occurred to me, simply and strongly, that this infant was my sister; that if our birth order had been reversed, I might be the infant, held by her, trying her patience as she was now trying mine.

It was a tiny thought, but it brought with it that calm feeling of perspective and the personal nothingness that resides within it. It was a feeling of respect, of reverence for a glorious tiny daughter of God, and of worship for our common Father. It was a feeling I love and long for, but one I often forgot as I forged on to those exasperating days when I was insisting that my opinion was the right one when Saren became a teenager. Oh, that we could remember our nothingness as parents, and that our children are often smarter than we think and that they will listen more humbly themselves if they feel our humility. Then we would know even more surely that family and parenting and commitment and unity ARE the most important things in the world and in eternity.

Backup

The natural-consequence joy and blessings that flow naturally from humility, particularly the non-compelled kind (because that is the kind that takes the hardest thought and the most deliberate pursuit), have not only been recognized by prophets, but by sage thinkers from all walks.

C. S. Lewis said, "As long as you are proud you cannot know God. A proud man is always looking down on things and people: and, of course, as long as you are looking down, you cannot see something that is above you."[3]

G. K. Chesterton said, "How much larger your life would be

if [you] could become smaller in it. . . . You would break out of this tiny . . . theatre in which your own little plot is always being played, and you would find yourself under a freer sky, in a street full of splendid strangers."[4]

An anonymous writer said, "One sees great things from the valley; only small things from the peak."

And another, "The smaller you are, the bigger the things He can do to you and with you."

And Chesterton came at it one more time, possibly with a chuckle, "Without humility, it is impossible to enjoy anything, even pride."

Indeed, until we learn to see ourselves as small as we really are, it is hard to see other things as large and beautiful as they really are—and hard to see the full extent of God's power and Christ's glory as our Creator and Savior. But when our nothingness allows us to find such perspectives, they inevitably bring unity and dispel the Five Ds. And nowhere is this as important (or as difficult) as in our families.

With this nothingness comes not only worship and peace, but a gratitude for the larger sweep of the mystery and magic of what we cannot yet see or understand. As we practice this kind of humility in our homes, it will ultimately carry over into our wards and our world.

The Mental Health of Nothingness

The smaller we see ourselves, the less stress and pressure we feel, and the more perspective we have on the depression and anxiety we all experience.

We write parenting books, attempting to offer advice and ideas to families. Yet the best parenting we have ever done is when we didn't have an answer—when the scope or worry of an issue with one of our children reminded us of our inadequacy and of how little we knew and how we were, in fact, children trying to raise children. Many times, within that nothingness, we have been able to offer a unique form of prayer, essentially talking as babysitters to the true parent (who we know loves and knows those babies infinitely better than we) and asking that we might do as He would do, that we might know what He would do and what He would have us do. He then manifests, through impressions, answers, and inspiration, His love to His children who are our children and to His children who are us.

The most spiritual kind of mental health comes not from the false confidence (and hidden doubts) of a "can-do" attitude, but from the faith of a "can't-do-alone" attitude that opens us to the ultimate confidence of what He can do through us.

How (Again) and Conclusion

So, if the personal paradigm of nothingness is the answer to the first "how" of obtaining unity, it raises the next *how* question: How do we get—*really* get—that powerful but illusive quality of nothingness?

At least one answer is almost shockingly simple: Through praise!

Let us pose a series of questions that will back us into this answer: Why do scriptural prophets spend so much time, effort, and words praising God? Does God really need our praise? Why is such a large chunk of scripture devoted to often-repetitive Divine praise? Couldn't that scriptural space be better used in teaching us other gospel doctrines? Why are thirty-four of the songs in our hymnbook about praising God? (Second most of any topic, second only to Jesus Christ.) Why is *hallelujah* (which literally means "praise God") such a common word both in ancient scripture and in today's religious music? Why is praising God so practiced and so preached by prophets?

There is one simple and intriguing reason: Praising God is what causes us to, in the words of King Benjamin, "Remember, and always retain in remembrance, the greatness of God, and your own nothingness" (Mosiah 4:11).

Every time we consciously praise God—in song, in prayer, in the reading and quoting of scripture, in quiet pondering or solitude, in seeing and giving thanks for His bounty and His beauty—every time, we are making ourselves aware of and reminding ourselves, and remembering His "everythingness" and our nothingness. It is not because God needs it; it is because we need it.

It is that praise that causes the remembrance of nothingness, which then brings the non-compelled humility, which in turn yields the seventeen incredible blessings of family and unity, which brings to pass peace and joy today and exaltation tomorrow.

Now that is a series of connections worth pondering.

It's a high bar, it's a long road, it's an eternal goal that is not for the fainthearted, but we *have* eternity to lay hold on this gift we generally call humility and specifically call nothingness, and to develop and build this UNITY with each other and of our spirits with His. And once we get on the path, stretched and distant though it seems, we will feel ourselves moving ever so gradually—but sometimes in satisfying, soul-expanding bursts—toward the seventeen promises and the powerful unity that Benjamin promised could come to us and to our families.

THE UNITY AND STRONG FAMILIES OF "NOTHINGNESS"

What do we need to stay the course? Not everything . . . but nothing.

Christ's metaphor was children, and the development of non-compelled nothingness should start in our families, where we understand that both we and our children are children. And since families are the basic unit of the Church as well as of society, in our nothingness pursuit, we will be doing our small but important part in countering those dastardly Five Ds and fostering that one big U within our wards, our stakes, and the Church at large.

Discussion Questions and Personal Application

1. In what ways do pride and humility have opposite effects on unity within families?
2. Do you believe that an attitude and awareness of our "own nothingness" can actually produce the seventeen promises quoted here from Mosiah 4?
3. How can you experiment upon the premise that praising God is the sure path to non-compelled humility?
4. How might the perspective of nothingness influence how we pray?
5. Can you think of an example, either real or hypothetical, of how recognition of God's "everythingness" could make a difference in how you parent your children? How you treat a stranger? How you feel about those with whom you disagree?

The Power of Proximity

BEN SCHILATY

BEN SCHILATY works as an Honor Code administrator and adjunct professor at Brigham Young University in Provo, Utah. He is the author of *A Walk in My Shoes: Questions I Am Often Asked as a Gay Latter-day Saint* and cohosts the podcast *Questions from the Closet*.

A few years ago, I was asked to give a fifth-Sunday lesson in my ward on ministering to LGBTQ+ Church members. I had done tons of lessons like this in other wards and stakes, but this was the first time my own ward had invited me to speak on the topic. I usually feel confident and calm speaking to a group of strangers about my life, but this time I felt oddly nervous. I knew these people, and they were about to know a whole lot more about me. After my lesson I would continue being in this ward, so what I said and shared really mattered.

After the lesson, my bishop gave me a huge hug and said, "Thank you, brother. We needed that message." Then one of his counselors came up to me in tears and also gave me a hug. This was a man I knew. We'd sat in ward council together and chatted in the foyer and I knew his wife and his children, so as he spoke, I knew his words weren't hollow. He became visibly emotional and said, "I am so glad my kids get to grow up in a ward that you're a part of."

As a gay Latter-day Saint, I've often felt like I don't fit in. And I've felt like a burden, too. This is baggage that I still sometimes carry. When this leader told me that I was a gift to his family, he metaphorically grabbed that old baggage and tossed it away. I don't know if he had any idea at that moment, or since, what a positive impact his sincere expression of gratitude would have on me. That moment that impacted both of us so deeply only happened because I was able to share my heart with him and he was willing to listen, learn, and see what was inside.

Sister Sharon Eubank's October 2020 general conference address spoke to the pain of seeing problems in the world. She said, "This world isn't what I want it to be. There are many things I want to influence and make better. And frankly, there is a lot of opposition to what I hope for, and sometimes I feel powerless."[1] As she said this, she became visibly emotional and I thought, *I know that feeling, Sister Eubank.* Like her, I often wonder why it can feel so hard to do something good, even in the Church.

Then in true Sister Eubank fashion, she directed our focus to the power we all have to create a better world. She taught, "We may not yet be where we want to be, and we are not now where we will be. I believe the change we seek in ourselves and in the groups we belong to will come less by activism and more by actively trying every day to understand one another. Why? Because we are building Zion—a people 'of one heart and one mind' [Moses 7:18]."

That's it. That's part of the secret to creating a better world—building Zion by trying every day to understand one another. My bishopric member and I were both blessed as he took the time to understand my life. I was blessed because I felt seen, and he was blessed because he got to see one of God's children.

A few years earlier, I had a life-changing moment as a student at Brigham Young University. I sat in a blue chair in the Marriott Center, fixated on our forum speaker, activist and author Bryan Stevenson. His message centered on creating a more just society, and I could feel myself transforming as he spoke. "Our power is waiting for us, if we get proximate," he said. "We have to get closer to those places [where people are suffering] if we're going to change the world."[2] The invitation sunk deep into me, and I felt the Spirit testify that what he was saying was true.

A few hours after the forum, I arrived at class early. I was in my second year of my master's degree in social work, eager to graduate and change the world. Sitting alone in the classroom was a classmate of mine who had recently mentioned in passing that she had benefitted from Deferred Action for Childhood Arrivals (DACA), meaning that she had been brought to the United States as an undocumented minor. Inspired by the forum, I asked her if I could ask a few questions about her experiences as a DACA student, also known as a Dreamer. She was so happy to open her heart and told me that she had been brought to the United States as a baby and didn't even know she was undocumented until she was a teenager. My heart grew as I got proximate to a friend whose life was so different from my own. And I felt guilty for having sat in classrooms with her for more than a year without ever asking deep questions about her life. Then she said, "You're the only person besides my husband and family who knows any of this. No one else has bothered to ask." An hour later when class was over, she turned to me as she walked out the door and said, "Thank you for asking about my life. It means a lot to me."

Vulnerability and openness are contagious. This friend later saw on Facebook that I was going to an event for LGBTQ+ BYU students. She messaged me and asked if she could come with me. Of course! I was so thrilled she wanted to learn about me and my life! I had stepped into her shoes, and now she wanted to step into mine.

I came to know a few other Dreamer students at BYU. Two of them were talking to me about my experiences as a gay Latter-day Saint, and after sharing so much about myself, I asked about them. Once again, I stepped into experiences that were very different from my own. As they talked about the legal issues and their uncertain futures, I began to feel powerless. I finally asked, "So how can I help you and other Dreamers at BYU?"

One of them said, "You can learn more."

That's all she asked: that I learn. She recommended two books written by undocumented immigrants that I quickly purchased and read. They were soul-expanding. How had I been so unaware of these experiences before?

This word kept bouncing around in my head: *proximity, proximity, proximity.* Then, just like Sister Eubank expressed, I noticed things in the world that I wanted to make better, but I wondered what power I could possibly have to solve these huge problems. But I wasn't powerless. I knew the answer. Proximity.

As an administrator and professor at BYU, I recently developed and taught a course titled "Understanding Self and Others: Diversity and Belonging." As part of the class, each of my students had the assignment to interview two people whose backgrounds differed from theirs and write an essay on what they learned. I trained them on how to conduct these interviews because I wanted my students to approach others with humility and respect, and with their permission. This is what I taught them:

First, ask for the person's consent. "Is it okay if I ask you some questions about your experiences as a Black Latter-day Saint?" If they agree, start with a "grand tour" question that allows them to take the conversation in any direction they want. "What's it like being a woman in America?" "How has being gay affected your life?" "Why did you decide to immigrate to the United States?" "Could you help me understand what it's like to have a disability?"

On the day we practiced doing proximity interviews in class, I jumped from one group to another to observe how they were doing. I felt like an intruder as I popped into deeply personal conversations. I was amazed that my students were being so vulnerable with each other so quickly. Simply asking sincere, open-ended questions created the space for students to share their hearts. Class that day felt like a sacred space. As we debriefed, I asked one student what the experience had been like. She became emotional and said, "It felt really good to feel understood. I needed that today."

Grading papers is literally the worst part of teaching, so I didn't anticipate the level of emotion I would feel as I read through my students' proximity papers. Almost all of them interviewed people they already knew, and again and again students wrote things like, "I assumed X about my best friend, but it was really Y," or, "I thought I knew them well, but now I know them so much better," or, "We planned to talk for twenty minutes but chatted for three hours." My students realized that there was so much below the surface in these established relationships that they hadn't seen until they asked. Asking good questions and pausing to listen helped them understand the people in their lives in new and deeper ways. I have permission to share two brief stories.

One student wrote, "I was lucky enough to be able to interview my own mother for this. My mom is my hero. I truly look up to her more than anyone. Her experience is unique and messy, interesting and complicated. I know about her situation, but because it is messy, it can be hard to recall details. What I didn't know, though, were my mom's thoughts and feelings on her identity." Her mom is gay. She had known this about her mom for years as a fact—as a descriptor. Through this assignment, my student came to see some of the many ways that this reality has impacted her mom's life. Just knowing a fact about a loved one doesn't mean that they are truly known to us. That takes real work. She continued, "I learned things about my mom I didn't know. I feel a little sad that I didn't know these things before."

Another student also interviewed his mom, who had immigrated to the United States before he was born. He wrote, "I learned that I am a product of many blessings and sacrifices and that it's hard to give up your homeland and the family that are still there. It's no laughing matter the sacrifice immigrants make to provide opportunities for their family and children." Although he grew up knowing that his mom had immigrated, he had never really taken the time to understand the impact of her choice to leave her home country. He moved beyond knowing a fact about his mom to knowing her story.

It is important to actively cultivate empathy with genuine curiosity when hearing another person's story. As someone speaks to me, I try to ask sincere follow-up questions, and then listen some more. I don't try to fix their problems or offer counsel, but just listen and let their realities sink into me. Over time, I've learned to ask some good questions: What do you wish people understood about your identity? Could you describe some of your most interesting experiences? What do you wish people would ask you?

What have you not been able to share that you would like to share?

When the Savior visited the Nephites, He invited a multitude of 2,500 people to feel the marks of the Crucifixion on His body so they individually could know that He was their Savior. This they did "one by one" (3 Nephi 11:15). I don't know how long these individual interactions took. I don't know what words were exchanged. But I do know that they saw Jesus and He saw them. I have often thought that I don't have time to learn so many individual stories. I don't have time to walk in everyone's shoes and see life through their eyes. But Jesus had the time. And His visit ushered in generations of peace. If I want to be like Him, I at least need to try to see each individual and to let them see me.

My bishopric sincerely sought to understand me. They peeked into my heart and then thanked me for opening it up to them. Those sincere expressions of love and gratitude for me were powerful because they came right after they had heard my story. They weren't grateful for a random ward member; they were grateful for me—Ben Schilaty. Sister Eubank and Bryan Stevenson are right. The way to make positive change in the world is to actively try to understand other people and get close to them and their experiences. Zion isn't built with a hammer. It is built with a yoke. Zion is built as we get proximate to others and share their burdens. It is built as we listen, share, and seek to understand. We build Zion when we actively knit our hearts together (see Mosiah 18:21).

Discussion Questions and Personal Application

1. Who has helped you feel seen and heard? How and when did that happen?

2. How does getting to know the hearts and minds of those around us build the kingdom of God?
3. What examples have you found in the scriptures and Church history of disciples of Christ seeking to understand one another? What did they do well? How can you apply what you've learned to people currently in your life?
4. Who in your congregation would you like to get to know better? Why?
5. What group of people do you know little about? How could you learn more about them?
6. How would you like to share your heart with your friends, loved ones, and community? What is holding you back and what would help you overcome it?

The Juxtaposition of Unity and Sameness

NEYLAN McBAINE

NEYLAN McBAINE is the founder of the Mormon Women Project and Better Days 2020. As an advocate for women, she is the author of *Women at Church: Magnifying LDS Women's Local Impact* and *Pioneering the Vote: The Untold Story of Suffragists in Utah and the West*.

When I declared to urban Latter-day Saint friends at age thirty-three that I was leaving my hometown of New York City to move to Utah, I was mostly greeted with warnings: Didn't I know that I would writhe under the expectations of conformity there? That my unique identity as a working mother who had only ever lived in apartments in New York, San Francisco, and Boston would be squelched? How did I expect to raise free-thinking children in unimaginative uniformity?

Being a member of the Church in major metropolitan coastal cities had certainly been an education in the diversity and variety of our heavenly parents' children. I loved this about my city upbringing and young-adult years. I loved dancing to the salsa music at stake youth dances, selected by the members from Spanish

THE JUXTAPOSITION OF UNITY AND SAMENESS

Harlem. I loved having new Black members of the Church join the ward choir and show us how worship music should *really* sound. I loved how my wards mixed single people with large families, the wealthy with those struggling to get by, the newly baptized person of color with the Pioneer descendant.

When I went to the temple for the first time, I embraced the idea that "beauty and variety" are built into the earth's creation. This phrase, said early in the narration depicting the flora and fauna of the Creation, stands out to me no matter how many times I attend an endowment ceremony. I feel the truth contained in that phrase every time: the range of design of God's creations is a feature, not a bug. A bird's beauty may be good for nothing except to bring us joy. A flower's intricacy may not serve any purpose other than to radiate a different color than its neighbor. And that's the way God wants it.

Other areas of my life have also supported the principle that both beauty and variety are essential in God's creations. In my love of music, I studied the power of dissonance and unexpected chord progressions to drive a musical theme. Modulating keys, contrasting tempos, and juxtaposed styles are the hallmarks of moving and memorable music. In my love of literature, I studied the power of conflict to drive a plot. Placing characters in unexpected and often trying circumstances is the very formula that drives personal growth and narrative direction.

I have a testimony of "beauty and variety." Perhaps more importantly, I have a testimony that they go together. That beauty is variety. That variety is beauty. That beauty + variety = God's will. And that this pairing is one of the fundamental guiding principles that guided the creation of this earth.

It is not, then, a stretch for me to believe that the beauty of variety is in fact a fundamental principle that guided the creation of God's human children, too. And the truth is that my years in Utah have definitely been lacking in the kind of variety of people that I loved about my urban experiences. The cultural richness of my youth is not here. I miss that feeling of coming together with people who have very different socioeconomic circumstances or life experiences and knowing that our love for the gospel of Jesus Christ is enough to bring us together. When your Utah ward consists of your neighborhood and thus the people who have the education, economic standing, and aesthetic priorities to live on your street, the opportunity to bump elbows with worshippers different from yourself is much harder to find.

This outward uniformity among worship congregations in the geographic heart of the Church would suggest that my friends were right all those years ago when they warned me about moving to Utah: that because wards in Utah are more consistently made up of people who share cultural and socioeconomic expectations, we would think and act similarly. They were, in fact, wrong.

Ironically, my years in Utah have presented me with a much *greater* challenge to finding common ground with my fellow Saints. Even though we look much more alike and share cultural backgrounds, there are deep-seated and fundamental variances to the way we approach life that are invisible, obscured by the seemingly uniform appearance. I have found it much harder to feel unified with those who look like me and live on my street than those with whom I appeared to have little cultural connection.

Perhaps I am deceived by the uniform appearance of my neighbors, primed to think we should be more similar than we are and thus more disappointed when we are not. Perhaps I am blinded by the socioeconomic and stylistic similarities, thinking they are indicators of political, educational, and spiritual harmony as well. As it is, I find myself more eager to embrace a new convert in Harlem or a member wearing jeans to church in San Francisco than I do my own Utah neighbor with whom I disagree about attitudes and opinions.

If I truly believe that beauty is variety and variety is beauty, I need to believe it about the unseen differences as well as those that are seen. I have been working on this, and progress is slow. As for many people, our current political landscape has been a wake-up call for me. As a New Yorker from the 1980s, I knew Donald Trump as a parodied figure from the local gossip columns. In 2016, I didn't have a single childhood friend who voted for Trump for president. Many did not even know anyone else who had voted for him. Meanwhile, among those in Utah who looked more like me and held religious convictions like me, the reactions to Trump's victory were wildly varied and much less consistent. People who lived on my street and who I was related to revealed an unseen variety that took me by surprise. Was this variety also beautiful?

I was unprepared to give as much weight to variety of opinion as I was to the variety of external cultural markers. But I don't get to pick and choose what kind of diversity is acceptable and desirable and what I wish to obscure. If variety is beauty, as I believe it is, then the responsibility is on me to align myself with God's vision of creation. It is up to me to find the beauty in that variety, even if—and maybe especially if—I have to look particularly hard.

Discussion Questions and Personal Application

1. What elements of your life demonstrate that variety results in beauty? How do you define beauty?
2. When have you been surprised that someone who seems

similar to you is actually very different? How did you respond to this realization?
3. Have you ever been able to create a truly meaningful connection with someone who seems different from you? What allowed you to create that connection?
4. Have there been times in your life when you wish those around you were more similar to you? How have you pushed back against that impulse?
5. What methods do you use to gain insight into others' values and priorities? How do you learn deeply about them?

Divine Diversity

MARK ESTY

MARK W. ESTY has a BS in applied physics, an MS in mechanical engineering, and an MBA from Brigham Young University. He currently works as an operations manager and lives in Celebration, Florida, with his wife, Melanie.

As we analyze the world around us, we can gain insights into the Lord's intentions and perspectives. One of the many names for Christ is the Light of the World. The fortuitous homophone of sun/Son in English helps to remind us that the sun is a type of Christ. It is the center of our solar system; without its gravitational presence, the structure of the solar system would fall into chaos, and without its light and energy, all living things would die. As we consider the concepts of unity and diversity, I find it interesting that while each individual photon abides by divine laws governing speed and composition, the sun emits light or energy in a nearly infinite span of wavelengths. This incoherent light includes a full range of frequencies that join together to create beautiful rainbows and pure, white light while the additional wavelengths of electromagnetic radiation add energy and heat to the earth.

The world illuminated by this sun was created with an incredible diversity of plants, insects, animals, and landscapes. It was then populated by children of God who are as infinitely diverse physically, emotionally, and spiritually as the wavelengths of light from the sun. The Son who implemented God's vision for creation clearly gloried in diversity and saw no contradiction between this variety and the unity of their purpose. Inherent in this love of diversity is a respect for the individual nature and agency of all intelligences. Our heavenly parents rejoice in our individual natures while encouraging us to join with them in creating pure, diverse, unified light and truth.

Confidence and Diversity

In contrast, Lucifer and his followers feared this diversity and its potential consequences. Lucifer's plan is one of conformity without deviation. The freedom inherent in a diversity of thoughts, actions, choices, and personalities contains within it the possibility of failure and pain.

In theory, Lucifer's plan would have eliminated the risk of failure by guaranteeing an identical outcome, but it would, of necessity, have required a singular path. The diversity inherent in the Father's plan would have been eliminated, subjugated to the monotony of singularity.

In my view, a sun that represented Lucifer's plan would emit a single monochromatic wavelength of light, essentially a laser. Picture a room illuminated by only a single color (such as a red light bulb). All objects would be visible as only shades of this one color. From this perspective, Lucifer's plan may have resulted in a single species of bird, a single grain to eat, a single type of tree, and human beings who all resembled one another and acted identically.

We can assume that a being who fears the risks and consequences of diversity would be incapable of glorying in and appreciating the beauty of diversity in any form. It would also be easier for such a being to maintain power, to control and guarantee outcomes, without the complex environment arising from variety and choice.

The corollary to this is that the incredible diversity in nature is a demonstration of the true Creator's personal confidence and optimism, which allows Him complete comfort even within an infinitely diverse environment. This provides some insight into Christ's and our heavenly parents' characters. Their confidence and security in Their own characteristics and knowledge allow Them to not be threatened by or fear the unknown. They know Their place in the universe; They know the laws of the universe; They know the consequences of violating those laws. This confidence provides Them with the freedom to allow dissension and diversity without fear.

The Motivation of Fear

Why did so many of our heavenly siblings follow Lucifer? Why would they choose a monochromatic, monotone world after just viewing the technicolor vision presented by their Father and Eldest Brother? While pride and a desire for power were essential motivations of those who led the rebellion, fear was likely a dominant motivation for many of the fallen souls: fear of their own inadequacies, fear of the choices of others, fear of the unknown, fear of the apparent chaos in a diverse world.

How often do we find ourselves nurturing these same fears?

How often does our motivation when criticizing or condemning others arise from a fear of how their choices and actions will impact us or things that are important to us?

Whenever we are tempted to criticize or condemn another person, we should check our motivations and our intentions. Are we motivated by fear? Are we attempting to control their actions and therefore control the consequences of their actions? If we are, then we are following in the footsteps and philosophy of Satan and not our elder brother Jesus Christ.

Whenever Christ chastised anyone, He did it out of deep love and concern for the individual and his or her salvation. The Savior's reproof always came from a place of love for the sinner and respect for agency. Are we as careful when we reprove?

Fear and Leadership

Throughout history, fear, anger, and hate have been cheap shortcuts used by false leaders to gain followers and power. If leaders succeed in arousing one of these emotions in their followers and directing this emotion at an external target, they obtain "puppet strings" they can use for manipulation and control.

This is the mechanism Hitler and modern terrorist leaders have used to turn the fear and anger of their followers toward the Jews and other religious groups. Religious leaders seeking power identified "witches" and "heretics" throughout the ages. In the Book of Mormon, Amalickiah sought to expand his power by inciting the Lamanites to anger against the Nephites (see Alma 47). We see this same methodology in modern politicians on all sides. I would suggest this as a powerful litmus test for a politician or any leader: Do they succumb to the temptation to lead by fear? Sadly, I have rarely seen a major politician in the last several decades, on any side, who is able to resist this temptation.

Outside of politics we can see this same temptation in our own lives. I spent several years working in door-to-door sales. My friends and family frequently joked that I was selling my soul for money. I believe that selling is an important aspect of a smoothly functioning economy and can be as ethical as any profession. However, early on in my sales career, I observed that many of the experienced people who I admired as honest individuals were allowing their ethics to slowly slip and degrade. I sought to understand the mechanism for this degradation. As I sought an answer through observation and prayer, I came to believe that a significant common thread was leadership by fear. It is common in sales to encourage fear and present a product as the solution to that fear: the security salesman who emphasizes all the recent burglaries in the area, or the pest-control saleswoman who encourages your fear of spiders or cockroaches. The fear of losing a great deal if you don't buy immediately. I came to see that even when all the facts are true, selling with fear has a negative impact on the character of the salesperson and on the experience of the customer.

How often do we use fear as a motivator in our homes, in church, and in our community discussions? At the core, Satan's methods have varied little over time. The same fear that served his purposes in the premortal life is a tool he encourages among the righteous and the unrighteous in this life. If we find ourselves being motivated by fear or seeking to motivate through fear when discussing salvation, immigration, the climate, the economy, or what our child should eat for dinner, we should immediately stop and challenge ourselves and our motives.

Does this mean that real dangers, risks, and threats do not exist? No. Prophets throughout history have warned us of dangers and serious consequences. The error is not in the content but in the motivation and emotion tied to the delivery. When we teach with the Spirit, both the speaker and the hearer are "edified and rejoice together" (D&C 50:22). If we are not feeling the Spirit and gaining knowledge and edification from the discussion, then we are in the wrong, even if our facts are 100% correct.

President Boyd K. Packer said, "Fear is the opposite of faith."[1] If we ground our discussions in faith rather than fear, we will experience unity even when we disagree. We can also find that we will become more persuasive (or persuaded) when an atmosphere of faith and hope exists within us and within our interactions.

One of the most influential and powerful discussions in my life came from this type of edifying conversation, which could have led to a very different outcome. From observations and discussions with family, I had determined that my mother had some false viewpoints and opinions that were negatively impacting her and others. While I was confident in my perceptions, I spent significant time pondering and praying on how to share my feedback. Even though my mother could have perceived the opening of the conversation as an attack, she instead chose to enter a dialogue, ask questions, and provide answers. I entered the conversation as a teacher, and I left as a student. It was from this conversation that I came to understand the incredibly negative impact of emotional abuse. I learned that abuse is rooted in fears that drive abusers to seek control over another person. Most importantly, I learned that abusers are not a separate species. All of us, myself included, contain the potential to become abusive and harm those we love if we surrender to our fears and the corresponding desire to control those closest to us.

At the time, I assumed that the epiphanies from this conversation would be enough to prevent me from falling into patterns of fear and control. I was wrong. After my next failed relationship, I was able to look back and see that my fears and my corresponding desire for control had undermined the relationship. Intellectually learning the concepts was relatively easy, but applying them into my life was much more difficult. This conversation was instrumental in helping me to prepare for marriage, and I still reference it regularly as I evaluate my choices and actions. If I had neglected this conversation to avoid confrontation, or if I had approached the conversation without the support of the Spirit, my life and future relationships would likely have taken a very different path.

Respect for Agency and Diversity

We know that "charity is the pure love of Christ" (Moroni 7:47). We have also been taught that we should pray for and seek to develop this pure love. What does this attribute look like in practice? From the story of the War in Heaven we can observe that respect for individual characteristics and desires has been an essential part of the plan from the beginning. Our Heavenly Father and Jesus Christ know the one and only path to exaltation, but They also know that the end goal requires us to change our natures—to become, not just to arrive at a destination. They recognize that a soul who is coerced and controlled will always be miserable. Their pure love is large enough to allow us to choose damnation as well as exaltation. Even more impressive, Their humility is great enough to recognize that we all have different strengths and weaknesses. As such, we will all traverse unique paths if we are to have the hope of learning and overcoming. Once again, we see that They are confident in Their knowledge of the beginning and the end. They know the essential components and ingredients of a divine soul and They will, respectfully, do all They can to help us achieve our individual potential, if that is the deep desire of our souls.

In situations where we find ourselves uncomfortable or unwilling to respect the agency of others, we should investigate our own personal confidence and knowledge. Are we willing to love them enough to respect their choices, their desires, and their unique paths? Do we trust that the Lord has done, and will do, all that He can to guide and encourage them just as He has for us? Do we make ourselves available to act in love when moved upon by the Spirit? As we navigate this difficult balance, we must remember that respecting the agency of others does not necessitate the abandonment of truth. In fact, the confidence to respect the agency of others can only stem from the knowledge and confidence in unchanging eternal laws and their consequences. At the same time, we can also trust that our vision is narrow and finite. How often do we arrive at far-reaching conclusions about the final state of another's soul based on simplistic assumptions?

Learn by Observation

We are literal children of our heavenly parents and therefore have similar characteristics and attributes within us. We can learn a great deal by observing the choices our Father in Heaven and His Son made when creating this world and by observing our own instinctive reactions to these creations. I am amazed by the universality of our deep and innate responses to beauty as well as our love of new discoveries.

We can strive to grow our ability to appreciate and respect the diversity of others. If we increase our confidence in God's plan and in our place within that plan, then we have no need to fear, hate, or be angry with others. If we remain rooted in love and choose faith rather than fear, the discord will not exist inside us. Others may choose to be angry with us. They may choose to attack or condemn us. But if we reject anger and choose love, we will be able to safely walk out of the chaos and destruction like Alma and Amulek walked out of the prison in Ammonihah (see Alma 14:27–28).

We sometimes think of biased or closed-minded individuals as looking through tinted glasses that change their perceptions of the world around them. In these situations, they are willfully choosing to reject the infinite wavelengths of the Lord's light and truth and creating a personal world illuminated only by the singular wavelength of their choosing. If we desire to be a Zion people in a fallen world, we need to remove barriers that decrease our receptivity to divine light. We have been called and given the opportunity to choose celestial emotions and motivations in all our interactions and set the example of faith and love for our families and neighbors.

Discussion Questions and Personal Application

1. When was the last time you were angry at someone else's choice(s)? Why were you afraid of their choice(s)? Did you choose to criticize or attack? How did you show forth an increase of love and charity afterward, or how could you have done so?
2. Consider Lucifer's plan in the Council of Heaven. What aspects of his plan might sound appealing or persuasive? Why were we willing to trust our Father's plan despite the risks, dangers, and suffering?
3. How do we balance the oneness and diversity of divine union?

4. How are fear and anger toward the choices of others and a lack of faith in God related?
5. How can we speak truth and cry repentance to the world while retaining pure charity for even the most misguided acts or choices of our divine brothers and sisters?

At-One-Ment

BILL TURNBULL

BILL TURNBULL did his undergraduate and graduate studies at BYU, after which he began an entrepreneurial and consulting career. In 2016 he cofounded the Faith Matters Foundation (www.faithmatters.org), whose mission is to explore an expansive view of the restored gospel. He and his wife, Suzy, have six children and twenty-four grandchildren and live in Midway, Utah.

I discovered life's most profound truth in an obscure, outdated Latter-day Saint chapel built in the shadow of a beet sugar factory just east of Idaho Falls, Idaho. I was eighteen at the time and was home for the weekend from college. My nineteenth birthday and the expectation of applying to serve a full-time mission were looming on the near horizon. Despite a somewhat misspent youth, the idea of serving a mission had always appealed to me. The prospect of giving myself to some cause greater than my overly nourished ego seemed increasingly important.

I had been raised in a devout family in a somewhat self-contained Latter-day Saint community. I had in theory accepted the ideas that I belonged to God's true Church and that my generation was foreordained to take the gospel to the ends of the earth in preparation for Christ's return. But I knew I would need a serious change of heart to represent Christ and His Church without hypocrisy. Despite having occasionally recited the expected words of testimony during my youth, I had not lived a life of faith and had very little honest conviction of even the existence of God, let alone a testimony of the divinity of my church. And those two facts began to weigh heavily on me as I finally faced the reality of serving a mission.

I was home from college for the weekend and was in the midst of several days of fasting and prayer. As I took the sacramental bread in that little chapel, I began to feel a flood of love and deep acceptance enter my body, filling me with a joy and light I could never have imagined. My heart was ablaze with love, and I felt it flow out from me to the row of white-haired widows who sat in their accustomed pew in front of me. My ego seemed to dissolve in this moment, and love seemed to fill that little chapel and flow out the open windows into the world outside. Nothing had prepared me for this new reality God had shown me. I had no language for it at the time.

As I emerged from the church house after the meeting, the whole world seemed different. The trees and grass and sky seemed pulsating with life, and I felt deeply connected to all of it. My family and neighbors, religious or not, seemed to be walking around unaware that they were in reality lit angels, each a unique expression of a light that animated them all. The world no longer seemed divided to me. I could see clearly that we are fundamentally connected, despite how our thoughts might seek to divide us.

The pull of the world, including habits of thought, can be strong. Over the subsequent days and weeks, the scales that had fallen from my eyes slowly formed again, and I unwittingly returned to my divided world. But not entirely. The epiphany that we are all connected, which has been confirmed to me in both powerful and subtle ways since that day, is one of the few things I know for sure, because I experienced it. The light of Christ is in and through all things. And that light is love.

I once heard Dr. Rachel Naomi Remen retell a Jewish creation story, first told to her by her grandfather:

> In the beginning there was only the holy darkness, the Ein Sof, the source of life. And then, in the course of history, at a moment in time, this world, the world of a thousand thousand things, emerged from the heart of the holy darkness as a great ray of light. And then, perhaps because this is a Jewish story, there was an accident—and the vessels containing the light of the world, the wholeness of the world, broke. And the wholeness of the world, the light of the world, was scattered into a thousand thousand fragments of light, and they fell into all events and all people, where they remain deeply hidden until this very day.
>
> Now, according to my grandfather, the whole human race is a response to this accident. We are here because we are born with the capacity to find the hidden light in all events and all people, to lift it up and make it visible once again and thereby to restore the innate wholeness of the world. It's a very important story for our times. And this task is called *tikkun olam* in Hebrew. It's the restoration of the world.

We moderns are living too much in our heads—in our thoughts—and our hearts are failing us. The mind tends to divide; the heart tends to unite. Social media and cable news networks have perfected the very profitable science of training our brains to see outrage in the world and to confirm our biases. We unwittingly line up like pigs to be fed the daily slop served up at their troughs. We are living too much out of fear and suspicion of "the other."

The lovely young Bulgarian writer Maria Popova wrote:

> All human lives are too various and alive with contradiction to be neatly classed into the categories in which we try to contain the chaos of life, and yet we spend so much of our unclassifiable lives classing the lives of others. One measure of kindness might be the unwillingness to crush complexity into category, the refusal to lash others with our labels.[1]

She also wrote:

> It is a beautiful impulse—to contain the infinite in the finite, to restore order from the chaos, to construct a foothold so we may climb toward higher truth. It is also a limiting one, for in naming things we often come to mistake the names for the things themselves.[2]

Yet according to the Genesis story, the Gods themselves set this world in motion by naming things, by creating distinctions (light/darkness, day/night, land/sea, man/woman, the various flora and fauna). God even invites Adam to join in the process of naming. In doing so, I like to think God is teaching Adam to see variety as beauty. But, as Maria Popova points out, there is a downside risk to sorting the world into categories. The Indian sage Jiddu Krishnamurti said that once a child learns the word "bird," that child may never see a bird again in the same way.

The impulse to "name" people—to sort them into categories—is powerful. Upon moving to Midway, Utah, eight years ago, I sat as the newest member of my ward's elders quorum. I listened to a lively discussion and tried to get a sense of the character of my new quorum. I remember one of the senior members of the quorum making a comment that seemed to betray a rather rigid, dogmatic worldview. My first thought was, "We're probably not going to become good friends if that's how he looks at the world." But near the end of our meeting, when volunteers were sought for an assignment at the Church cannery, this brother's arm shot up. I sensed an opportunity and quickly raised my hand to snag the third and last slot.

In the hours we spent driving to the cannery and working our shift together, a funny thing happened. We became fast friends and forever brothers—even though we continue to view and experience the world rather differently. We created a one-ness through being and serving together that transcends the distinctions our minds try to serve up to us.

The same applies to our relationship to the natural world. To our ancient ancestors, creation was alive. They were aware of, and sustained by, the deep, unifying networks that comprise the natural world in which they were immersed. Moderns have set about to dissect the natural world into its constituent parts in service of scientific analysis and commercial exploitation. The result, of course, has been an explosion of discovery and technology—with its accompanying comforts and material prosperity. But in this headlong rush to improve our way of living, modern society largely lost sight of the fundamental connectedness and unity of all things. We are now paying a price for that myopia in the form of extreme environmental degradation, the ever-present potential of nuclear annihilation, and deep social division.

But we may be seeing a new day dawning. It's interesting that the same scientific enterprise that has been instrumental in creating both the blessings and curses of modernity may be showing us a path back to unity. We are learning surprising things about the deep intelligence and connectedness of the macro world (like forests and other ecosystems), and we're learning about perhaps even more surprising connections at the level of subatomic particles (discoveries like quantum entanglement). The secular age may be yielding to a recognition of an almost mystical reality—a fundamental connectedness of all things.

Our faith has always pointed to this deep intrinsic unity of all things and to the eventual restoration of that unity. That, to me, is the essence of the gathering project in which we are engaged—recognizing the brotherhood and sisterhood of every person who has ever lived on this earth, sharing the universal gospel of Jesus Christ, and eventually sealing all of humanity together. Jesus's great Intercessory Prayer expressed His vision and desire "that they may be one, even as we are one" (John 17:22). This is Christ's project of At-one-ment.

We can't really be Christ's partners in this work until we allow ourselves to feel deep in our hearts the fundamental unity of all creation, in all its blessed variety. We will have to do the soul-searching work required to transcend the distinctions our minds and cultures seem determined to impose upon us. We will need to come to see these differences as part of the variety and beauty of this world. Each of us will need to actively seek to transcend racial, political, religious, national, and other boundaries in order to gather these shards of light into one great whole. We will need to let our hearts train our minds to scan the world to see difference as beauty and wholeness rather than division.

As an eighteen-year-old in that little church house, my first powerful experience of divine love was something like a profound reverence for all things. Over time I have come to see love not only as a sense of deep connection, but as a desire to actively support the growth and flourishing of others, without expectation of result, and with a deep respect for the uniqueness of our paths. One-ness was never meant to be same-ness.

I've come to see At-one-ment as the process of understanding, and helping each other understand, that every creature, every human being, is animated by the Light of Christ and is therefore deeply interconnected. Only by realizing and living this fundamental truth can we mend a fractured reality and heal our wounding divisions. It is the great project of restoration.

Discussion Questions and Personal Application

1. How does the Ein Sof story told by Rachel Naomi Remen's grandfather help you see your role in both restoration and gathering differently? What might you do today or tomorrow to restore and gather?
2. Think about ways you sort people into categories and label them. How does it make you feel toward them?
3. It's easy to say that we value difference and diversity, but something about human nature keeps us from making the effort to actually appreciate, understand, and spend time with people quite different from us. It's uncomfortable. What are some "uncomfortable" practices you could adopt to open your heart and life to "the other"?

4. What are some practices you could adopt to help you see, understand, and feel the connectedness of the natural world? How might it change your way of being in the world?

One Heart and One Mind

ELIZABETH HAMMOND

ELIZABETH HALE HAMMOND, MD, is a professor of pathology and medicine at the University of Utah School of Medicine and an internationally recognized researcher in cardiac transplantation and cancer diagnostics. She and her husband, Jack, are the parents of three children and have twelve grandchildren.

During Jesus's final hours on earth, He gathered His Apostles and commissioned them to go into all the world to teach His gospel of universal love. In his Intercessory Prayer, He fervently asked God "that they all may be one; as thou, Father, art in me, and I in thee, that they also may be one in us" (John 17:21). That call for unity in the faith remains to this day, and it's worth pondering the ways in which we can achieve more unity.

We are living in an age of vitriolic opinions about serious issues of our times: How should we deal with gun violence? with immigration laws? with LGBTQ+ rights? Our responses to each of these concerns and many others is variable. We shout, shame, and ignore others rather than engage respectfully about thorny problems. Little progress in understanding or even dialogue results. We retreat to the company of our friends and listen only to those voices who support our positions. Do we work toward greater love and understanding? No! We fail because we are being sabotaged by our own thought processes, unaware of our hidden weakness, our biases.

To understand how serious biased thinking is and how hard it is to control, we need to understand how we actually think. Our brains have two modes of thinking: intuition and rational thought.

In almost everything we do, we use intuition to make decisions because it is fast and often accurate. Intuition can be accessed quickly because its conclusions are pre-formed from life experiences, religious (and other) education, and opinions of trusted individuals. Intuition helps us drive cars safely, guide our children toward adulthood, and navigate the activities of daily living or working without much forethought. While typically helpful, these pre-formed thoughts can also harbor cognitive biases, most of which we are unaware of. For example, when I see a young man on the street begging for money, that sight evokes biased opinions about that man's life and goals: *Is he there because of laziness or drug addiction?* I often made that assumption until I learned that mental illness and economic misfortune are more common causes of homelessness than sloth or addiction. Addiction is more often a consequence of mental illness.

Such biased thinking can be controlled only when we are aware of it and seek for truth. Each of us derives biased conclusions based on trusting the opinion of others or opinions we derive from our life experience. I cannot imagine being homeless because of mental illness, for example. *Why not just get medicine or counseling?* I would think. On further reflection, I realized that many people lack options for treatments due to poverty or circumstances. What if you don't understand why you have dysfunctional thoughts and you have no concerned friends or family to guide you to helpful resources? Often, we are unaware of the reasons behind our opinions unless we reflect carefully on why we think as we do.

By contrast, our capacity to rationally categorize information comes from careful deliberate scrutiny. When we use our ability to reason through a problem, we consider alternatives our intuitive thinking might dismiss, due to ignorance, fear, or disapproval. To activate our rational thoughts, we must constantly ask ourselves to consider evidence that conflicts with our pre-formed ideas: *How can I judge this man's motives when I know nothing about his life or even very much about causes of homelessness in my community?* I need to think of him as a fellow child of God and learn about his life and challenges, as the Savior did so many times.

While serving an inner-city mission in Salt Lake City, my husband and I were asked to help a seriously depressed single mother who was struggling with many challenges. She was losing her disability income because of failure to update state agencies about her situation in a timely manner. Her teenage son was in juvenile detention in Ogden, but she could not attend therapy sessions because she had no money for gas. Her young daughter was struggling to attend school and grow up in the neighborhood without any help from her mother. This poor woman was so miserable that she was reduced to rarely doing more than sitting in the dark watching TV. We struggled to understand her circumstances, thinking about how unprepared we were to address her challenges and wondering what she could have done differently to avoid her problems. In that moment, we remembered our promise to love and serve the one and reflected on our inherent biases about this situation. We took a step back to analyze her situation and acknowledge parts of her life beyond her control that may have led to her difficult circumstances. We quietly and consistently asked questions and listened to her, offering our service without knowing exactly what we could do. We were able to do that because we knew we were on the Lord's errand and had prayed for His help when we left the house that day, full of uncertainty and discomfort.

She had not communicated with the state because she had been in the hospital on a suicide watch for the previous three weeks. We went to the agency that had denied her income, taking with us documentation of her hospitalization. We decided that we could take her to see her son and learn of his situation, carefully listening to the counselors and to this mother and then praying that we could apply the right tools to improve the situation. Over the next few months, we struggled together, fighting bed bugs and seeking compassion from an unreasonable landlord. We became friends and rejoiced together when we finally found her other housing and services for her depression. In the end we managed to shift away from our biased thoughts by knowing and loving this woman and listening to the guidance we received through prayer and faithful action. If we use our faith in Christ's gospel to guide and modify our thinking, we can see others as He sees them. We can reach out to those around us, suspending judgment of their actions, their attitudes, and their life circumstances, and enjoy relationships of love and kindness.

When we rely on the biases that inform our intuition unconsciously, we are more likely to disagree or contend with others. Such thinking is responsible for our conflicting opinions about the seriousness of COVID-19 and other contentious political and societal issues so rampant in our day. Biased intuitive thinking creates our judgmental opinions of others based on attributes such as age, gender, body size, sexual orientation, or skin color. I faced such biased attitudes when I chose to become a physician at a time when almost all physicians were men. Based only on my gender and not on my ability, male physicians believed that I did not belong in medicine. Voting rights for women in America were denied for years, based on biased views prevalent for centuries. Biased intuitive thought processes were obvious even in the Savior's day. *How could an ignorant carpenter's son be our teacher and spiritual advisor?* the people wondered. *What ideas of such an uneducated man could be relevant to our religion or circumstances?* His radical ideas of loving everyone defied prevailing opinions based on the law of Moses and the Jews' personal experiences. Similarly, our intuitive thoughts betray us as we seek to become united. Often before we reach out to listen, to love, or to serve others, we unconsciously consult our biased, pre-formed ideas: *Do I care about this person? Are they worthy of my love or service? They are so lazy or sinful that my help will do no good. They are so wrong about everything that I do not need to listen to them. We cannot discuss this issue because we will never agree.*

We also need to be careful not to attribute our biased thoughts to personal revelation. Christ is unlikely to prompt us to bash a political party, participate in a violent demonstration, or support or transmit dishonest rhetoric. Ascribing such thoughts to personal revelation degrades the value and attributes of this precious gift. We need to carefully consider the circumstances of those promptings. Do those feelings direct us to fear or hate others? If we consider our actions or thoughts in the context of Christ's love for us, how could we believe that such promptings come from God? We know how to obtain spiritual help from God through faith, prayer, and deep reflection. In contrast to biased thinking, when we feel the Spirit, it is more like the beautiful light filling the chapel or the warmth and joy we feel as we participate in a choir, meditate in a beautiful garden, or work together in love in our ward, family, or job.

How can we achieve unity in the Church? While honestly seeking truth combined with humility and meekness can help us move beyond our biases and bring us closer together, there are times that we will still disagree. What then? At that point, we should come together through Christ's central message of love and service. Certainly, we all agree on that. It is the most important message we have. What if after seeking diligently to understand underlying issues, we still can't agree on gun control? What if we are still struggling with various social issues that we perceive very differently? Do we set them aside? No. God wants us to advocate for positions we feel strongly about—supporting us to rely on our abilities to puzzle out thorny issues in our minds. Such advocacy needs to be tempered by our willingness to listen and learn from each other. Always at these times, we need to continually ask ourselves: *What is the evidence that I am wrong? What is the basis for my opinions? Is there a middle ground that we can all support?* Active listening and dialogue about issues will help us find our way.

In 1786 it looked like the fledgling "United States" were remarkably disunited. Fifty-five delegates met in Philadelphia between May and September to consider their future. Not only did they reject the Articles of Confederation altogether and define a central government with power to operate; they produced the first written constitution of any nation in the history of the world—one that continues to be a model for nations everywhere. Surely, they were personally biased, as we would be, about the difficult decisions that they faced, and yet they managed to overcome many of those biased thoughts that separated them. How? They cared deeply about nationhood and they had been locked away eating, sleeping, and talking together for four months, during which time they came to know and respect each other. They considered it a strength rather than a weakness to change their opinions in response to honest dialogue. Their desire for unity was ultimately stronger than their desire to satisfy themselves. Christ and His Apostles then and now highly value our quest for unity: to become a Zion people. He desires for us to be one in purpose and in commitment to His gospel of love and service. That should be the strongest motivation of all.

Discussion Questions and Personal Application

Think of a time when you have strongly disagreed with someone (or imagine a hypothetical situation where you have serious discord with another person). Holding that image in your mind, answer the following questions:

1. What is your first thought about this person? Do you first "consider the source" and judge the person by outward appearance, style of communication, life circumstances? How does that habit interfere with honest dialogue? What is your judgment of them based on?
2. Do you seek to understand their position or strongly advocate your own?
3. Where does your opinion come from: trusted advisors, opinion leaders, your experience, thorough analysis of the topic? What if your opinion is based on faulty assumptions?
4. How can you look for shared realities with this person? Can you find an underlying shared reality?
5. Next time you find yourself in a disagreement, can you ask these questions and try to have a healthy suspicion of your own thinking?

An Optimistic Road from Contention to Unity

MELANEY TAGG

MELANEY TAGG has a BS in civil engineering from Brigham Young University. She is an educator by trade and an advocate in the public square for civility and unity. She is a member of the Community Levee Association and directs the Venn Diagram Project. She and her husband, Daren, live in northern Virginia and have seven children and fifteen grandchildren.

When Eve and Adam fell forward into mortality, the human family not only became separated from God; they also became separated from each other. Mortal versions of emotion and communication, not to mention mortal tendencies toward weakness and sin, made unity among humans an elusive thing. One need not look further than Adam and Eve's own family to see that the human condition is prone to conflict and division.

The Lord, in His mercy, blessed the human family—His family—with two great commandments: He invited us to love Him wholly, and also to love our neighbors. He beautifully taught that our neighbors, ironically, include our enemies. He

AN OPTIMISTIC ROAD FROM CONTENTION TO UNITY

charged us to love everyone without exception. I am extraordinarily optimistic that we can, in all our variety and with the Lord's empowering grace, more fully and beautifully live the second great commandment.

I live in Loudoun County, Virginia. During the summer of 2021, our community was a hotbed of contention, division, and rancor. Broadly there was vehement disagreement over masks and vaccinations, the addressing of racism in school curriculum, and policies about the treatment of our LGBTQ+ community, among other issues. I found myself very disturbed, not by the fact that there was such strong division and such varied opinions—after all, rational people, given the same set of information, can come to vastly different conclusions—but by the tone, anger, unkindness, and incivility that arose from those holding different points of view. School board meetings, newspaper articles, social media posts, and other private and public communications were filled with accusation, affront, insult, and hatred. There was more than enough finger-pointing and demonizing to go around. The better angels of our nature were difficult to see.

Much of this conflict coalesced around a state-mandated policy intended to protect transgender students. The policy was made publicly available for both review and public comment. The public comment sessions during school board meetings were sadly circus-like. Commenters on both sides of the issue spoke passionately and often caustically, aggressively, and insensitively. Advocates of the proposed policy often cited the protection of all children in our schools. Opponents felt vehemently that their own interests and those of their children were being ignored.

A small but mighty organization in Loudoun County, the Community Levee Association (CLA), has an interest in the flourishing of life for all community members, particularly those who live on the margins of society. We at the CLA hoped to bring some sort of civility—some common ground, existing overlap, and maybe even civil compromise—to the discussion. We enlisted the participation of good, measured people from each side of the issue. We met separately with each side, building trust between them and the CLA. We then brought both sides together. The meeting we held was extraordinary by any measure. Trust was built between all participants—those opposed to the policy, those in favor of the policy, and neutral CLA members. Once trust was established, each participant openly, respectfully, and candidly shared what their interest was in the policy. During this phase, we were listening closely for any already existing overlap between otherwise opposing sides. We then continued on to the final step: proposing ideas to improve the policy that represented the newly discovered overlap that existed between sides, sides that came originally to the table thinking they had nothing in common. This meeting ended with remarkable goodwill—handshakes, embraces, exchange of contact information, and friendship. It was beautiful and moving to witness. Later, these two groups agreed unanimously on eight improvements to the proposed transgender protection policy (privacy measures, capital improvements, continued addressing of related issues, and so forth). These eight items were shared with the school board. Two were proposed in the school board meeting where the policy was up for a vote, and one was in fact voted on and added to the policy. The process of watching division melt into cooperation was powerful and beautiful—and one that I'm optimistic can be repeatedly duplicated.

There is a simple mechanism, the Venn diagram, whose purpose is to discover ways in which two or more things are the same or different. A common application may be to compare two animals; for example, a dog and a cat (who are typically cast as archenemies). In their separate portions of the circles, cats and dogs would have many distinct traits, such as their sociable natures, the food they eat, and the sounds they make. But they share many essential characteristics, which would appear in the center of the Venn diagram: both are mammals, both can be very affectionate, and so on. While cats and dogs are different, they are also the same in basic and important ways.

As divine offspring of godly heavenly parents, we have immutable similarities with all other humans: we are children of God, we are literal spirit sisters and brothers, our stories of origin have the same roots. Additionally, every single person that ever walked the earth chose in the premortal existence to follow our Savior and Redeemer, Jesus Christ. If we were to draw a Venn diagram of any two people, these wonderful, powerful, beautiful identifiers would be right in the middle, each time. The outside areas of our circles will be full also, indicating our different experiences, appearances, life circumstances, and opportunities for learning, not to mention opinions, preferences, faith constructs, political philosophies, and on and on. That is right and good. Additionally, our diagrams are fluid—things in our lives and the lives of others change and morph and grow. The exercise of learning from others—listening to more fully understand them, and seeking to not only see how we are the same but also understand and come to appreciate and respect how we are different—is a holy one, perhaps even a divine one. I am optimistically convinced that when we remember the divinity of the other person, regardless of our differences (which may be extreme), we will discover that we overlap already. It's so critical that we not sacrifice unity by clinging so wholly to our views and opinions and causes that we forget that we are already in sync with our neighbor in the most divine ways. That knowledge then facilitates our efforts to come to understand them and learn more from them in conciliatory, trusting, and holy ways.

I'm optimistic that these principles can be applied to the most extremely divided issues. Perhaps those on opposite sides of immigration issues could find that they all value quality of life and can move forward on how best to achieve that. Perhaps those on opposing sides of education issues could first find that they all value children being happy, safe, and healthy, and those children having opportunities to learn and grow. Perhaps those on opposing sides of gun issues could find that they all value safety, peace, and protection. Finding first where we agree, where we overlap, and where we are the same allows us then to have new ideas revealed to us about how we might cooperate, collaborate, and perhaps even compromise. We can then move forward together in unity, respect, and trust, all the while staying true to who we are and what we value.

I'm also confident that these principles have broad and varied application: in the public square, in wards and stakes, and in marriages and families. I love to engage with and learn from a family I know whose son, after his full-time missionary service, decided to separate ties with the Church. At about the same time, he shared with his family that he was gay. It has been a blessing and a gift to watch this family (the rest of whom are fully active in the Church) continue to find beautiful middle ground together. Not only is their dear son fully welcome, of course(!), in their home and at their table; so are his partner and his friends. Not only does this family have happy discourse on neutral topics, but I have watched and learned as they have spoken openly of faith and the Church and gay culture and gay relationships—and a whole host of other issues that in many circles would create discord and result in contention or withdrawal. Because each side is open to this kind of learning and dialogue and engagement, their loving bonds are strong. Their middle ground is healthy and robust.

Additionally, we seem to have come to believe that certainty and surety in and of themselves are badges of honor. We say things like, "I've thought about this for a long time and have found that the right way is . . ." or, "I've come to the certain conclusion that . . ." What if we replaced that thinking with the notion that we always have growth ahead of us—more learning, more progress, more understanding? Perhaps then we could replace our potentially misplaced certainty with notions like, "I'd never thought of it that way before," or, "I used to think this but now I think that," or, "Thank you for helping me to see this issue more fully." We must reject the notion that triumph over our perceived opponent is a victory. True victory lies in coming to know and subsequently love our neighbor in all her differences and in all his variety.

President Dallin H. Oaks taught this with weighty clarity when, in the April 2021 general conference, an Easter Sunday, he charged us with the following: "On contested issues, we should seek to moderate and unify."[1] This sequence matters. Where there is contest, we need to look inward and do the hard work of discerning where and how we can moderate our positions and our views, holding on to that which we fundamentally value but fully acknowledging that there is much on which we can compromise or come to the middle. Maybe in clinging to the truth, we're clinging too much to everything we think. We could ask ourselves, *Where might I be wrong on this?* or, *How could I try to see this differently?* Maybe we could seek to more fully follow the Savior by learning to love each one, including and especially those who are different than we are. Maybe in our willingness to do the hard work of moderating, unity will more naturally follow. Building unity, which is divine, is ultimately more achievable if we personally are willing first to moderate.

In this quest for finding overlap, common ground, and unity, we often think we are succeeding by leaving certain topics or issues off the table. We rightly hope to live lives free of contention and rancor. Too often we believe that the best way to do that is to not speak of things that can typically be contentious. I propose that this is avoidance, not success (understanding, of course, that not all folks want to engage with moderation and unity). True success is when we can speak and listen freely in love and respect, with open ears and hearts, to those who see things differently than we do. If we only engage with those whose politics, faith, racial background, and life experiences are similar to ours, where is the growth? Where is the learning? Where is the richness of human experience and human connection? Where is the beauty of discovery of the divinity in everyone that we meet? While this approach of huddling only with like-minded folks may be contention-free, the unity it achieves is potentially shallow. The aim we could seek for instead is one where we could embrace our opponent, listen and learn from our adversary, thank those with whom we disagree for teaching us, and subsequently sit down together at the table of the Lord, peacefully and contention-free in all of our diversity. That is true unity. That is the oneness of which Jesus Himself speaks.

I am optimistic—optimistic that the commandment that the Lord gave us to love our neighbor is possible. Experience teaches me that the more I know, understand, and love my Redeemer, the more I long to know, understand, and love my neighbor. The beautiful irony is that when I seek to more fully know, understand, and love my neighbor, my capacity to more fully know, understand, and love my Redeemer is infinitely enlarged.

Discussion Questions and Personal Application

1. How are disagreement and contention the same? How are they different?
2. How can we as individuals and as a Church more fully live the second great commandment? How can we genuinely and deeply love those who are different than we are? Think of examples of where great love was exhibited in various types of differences: political, religious, racial, economic, gender, and so forth.
3. Is it possible that two people can have nothing in common? Is it possible for two humans to have a Venn diagram with an empty middle? What are some things that all humans share in common?
4. What is President Dallin H. Oaks asking us to do when he charges us to "moderate and unify" on contested issues? How can we do this while still holding fast to absolutes that we hold as core beliefs? Is the skill of becoming more moderate a strength or a weakness?
5. Does holding our opinions and views close and quiet bring true unity? When do we speak freely, and when do we keep our thoughts private? Do we avoid contention by only sharing ideas with like-minded people?
6. How can we really, truly understand another person? How can we more fully listen to learn? How can we learn to not only understand but also to respect and honor another in their differences from us?

Religion: How We Use It Makes a Difference

RONELL HUGH

RONELL HUGH holds an MBA from Brigham Young University and leads a product marketing and strategy team at a technology company in Utah. He is the founder and CEO of Breathing Inclusivity, which is focused on giving business leaders, mission-driven employees, and companies the tools they need to create meaningful change within their organizations. He and his wife, Briawna, have four children and currently reside in Highland, Utah.

As a child growing up in Germany, I learned what it meant to be in a community of unity. Hergenfeld is nestled in rolling hills and grape vineyards fifty-four miles west of Frankfurt. This town of just over five hundred people was and still is a multigenerational family community. The people were extremely accepting and welcoming of my family, who were the only Black family in the town and the surrounding area. My childhood consisted of attending a local German public school, speeding around the town as if it were our own private racetrack in our

RELIGION: HOW WE USE IT MAKES A DIFFERENCE

pedal go-karts, and eating at my godparents' German restaurant, which entertained hundreds of people from near and far.

The people were honest, candid, and kind. Our quaint little town thrived due to people just being themselves and everyone respecting one another for who they were. There wasn't any pretense needed. When conflict arose, people verbally, in ways that Germans do, hashed it out. Maintaining a community of mutual respect and friendship was and is still a mainstay of the community.

In 1986, my parents made the hard decision to move our family to the Raleigh, North Carolina, area. My stepdad, Charles, was a native of Knightdale, a small suburb just east of Raleigh. It was December 1986 when the plane touched down in New York City at LaGuardia Airport. This transition would be seminal for me and my siblings, given we were entering a new country and culture vastly different from our tiny village in Germany.

Fast-forward: I was eight years old and walking down our pebble stone driveway to the mailbox to collect the mail. When I got to the mailbox, I saw that there was a sticker with three letters on it—KKK. I had no idea what those three letters meant. I gathered the mail and ran back into the house to give it to my mom. I told her there was a sticker on our mailbox with the letters "KKK." I can still see my mom's face—horror, concern, sadness, and anger—all rolled into one. It was this experience that awakened me to the perception of the color of my skin.

As I've matured and grown spiritually, I've learned more about the history, rationalization, and justifications of my skin color being classified as deviant, sinful, and dangerous. Where did this come from? What drives people to consider those who look like me to be a threat, less than, apelike, and not human? What was the foundation that ignited this century-old hatred?

Many of these ideas can, unfortunately, be traced to a deliberate misinterpretation of scripture.

Religion Used to Divide Us

Religion has been around since Adam and Eve were formed and residing in the Garden of Eden. When the Lord created Adam, He gave a commandment, saying, "Of every tree of the garden thou mayest freely eat: But of the tree of the knowledge of good and evil, thou shalt not eat of it: for in the day that thou eatest thereof thou shalt surely die" (Genesis 2:16–17). Heavenly Father and Jesus Christ presented Adam and Eve with agency, "the ability and privilege God gives us to choose and to act for ourselves. Agency is essential in the plan of salvation."[1] This is a key part of the plan of salvation and religion today.

Religion has been a force for good, emboldening many faithful followers of Jesus Christ to walk with and to seek Him. It was religion that strengthened Hezekiah and Josiah to move forward with faith, demanding change amongst their people, who were deeply entrenched in the world's idolatry worship and seeking success at any cost. Merriam-Webster defines religion as "a personal set or institutionalized system of religious attitudes, beliefs, and practices." It's these attitudes, beliefs, and practices that make each religion unique. More precisely, it's the interpretation of these that influences how people live their religious beliefs.

For us, as members of The Church of Jesus Christ of Latter-day Saints, we believe the purpose of our religion is "to help all of God's children come to Jesus Christ through learning about His gospel, making and keeping promises with God (covenants), and practicing Christlike love and service."[2] These attitudes, beliefs, and practices are our foundation, and hopefully we focus our thoughts, words, and actions to fulfill this purpose.

Despite the good that comes from religious observance, sadly, bad emanates from it as well. There are countless accounts in which religion is used as rationalization and justification for treating others with disdain, cruelty, unkindness, hatred, and even death. We only have to look at the history of the world or turn to the news to see how religion is leveraged to wedge discord, discontent, and disharmony throughout the world.

If we search the scriptures, we don't have to look any further than the Pharisees and Sadducees. During Jesus Christ's ministry on the earth, He continuously faced heated, contentious interactions with the Pharisees and Sadducees. These two religious powers of the time constantly used their interpretation of the law of Moses to justify their treatment of others.

Jesus Christ engaged in a conversation with the scribes and Pharisees in which He highlighted that they "sit in Moses' seat" (Matthew 23:2). Living the law of Moses was how followers of Jehovah showcased their faith and devotion. This was prior to His birth and ministry. The Savior continued by stating, "Whatsoever they bid you observe, that observe and do; but do not ye after their works: for they say, and do not" (Matthew 23:3). His main point was, "All their works they do for to be seen of men" (Matthew 23:5).

Jesus Christ went on to call them hypocrites, meaning a person who puts on a false appearance of virtue or religion, because of how they are living the law of Moses. One of His final woes indicates this perfectly: "Woe unto you, scribes and Pharisees, hypocrites! for ye make clean the outside of the cup and of the platter, but within they are full of extortion and excess. Thou blind

Pharisee, cleanse first that which is within the cup and platter, that the outside of them may be clean also" (Matthew 23:25–26).

I believe Elder Quentin L. Cook might have been describing the Pharisees and Sadducees when he insightfully shared, "Gospel extremism is when one elevates any gospel principle above other equally important principles and takes a position that is beyond or contrary to the teachings of Church leaders. . . . If we turn a health law or any other principle into a form of religious fanaticism, we are looking beyond the mark."[3]

Despite the world's need for the Savior, Jesus Christ, who gave His life and committed the ultimate and eternal sacrifice for each one of our salvations, the Pharisees and Sadducees played a key indicting role driving Him to the cross. They fully believed their religious positions, to the extent they could not see Jesus Christ for who He was, the answer to the law of Moses. Their religion was their weapon. They used it against anyone they perceived to be a threat.

Religion was a cornerstone to the Pharisees and Sadducees much like it was to the European settlers of North America. This rich, vibrant land presented a new beginning for the settlers with dreams of creating new opportunities for themselves and their families. These settlers brought with them their religion, the Church of England, when they established the colony in Virginia in 1619. It was late August 1619 when the first enslaved people were brought by white settlers to the shores of Virginia, creating what would become centuries of religious rationalization.

The early settlers began proliferating a religious teaching to support and validate their right to enslave Africans. Christians unitedly leveraged the curse of Cain—the claim that when Cain killed Abel, his brother, God cursed him with black skin—and the curse of Ham as religious rationalization and justification for

RELIGION: HOW WE USE IT MAKES A DIFFERENCE

enslaving people of African descent. This religious attitude led to many actions over centuries in which enslaved people were treated as property and not human.

As we look back on history, we see the treatment of Black sisters and brothers is religious-centered and government-supported. The years of inhuman treatment mentally, verbally, physically, and emotionally were justified by religious beliefs. Religion was the catalyst and government was the enforcer in maintaining power and separation.

When I think about my eight-year-old self standing in the kitchen of my house watching my mom's reaction about the KKK sticker, I didn't realize what religion could empower people to do. I believed religion was the great unifier, equalizer, and connector of all God's children. I couldn't have imagined that my fellow sisters and brothers in Heavenly Father's eternal family could see me as not created in His image all because of their bias against the color of my skin. I still believe that religion can and should be a unifier.

My journey has opened my mind and heart over the last several years with the knowledge that our challenges with race or racism in and outside of the Church aren't a secular issue. It is and has always been based on religious rationalizations or justifications turned into weapons.

Today, we see the influence of religion weaponized amongst our members. I hear countless experiences along the Wasatch Front in Utah, where I reside, from my friends who are members, were members, and are of other faiths. Their stories cause my knees to shake as I listen to them share experiences. I see religion weaponized when friends sadly share about neighbors not associating with them or allowing their kids to associate with their kids because they are not members of our faith. I see religion weaponized when a member in my stake shares with my wife that she had never known members could belong to the opposite political party. I see religion weaponized when in my predominately Latter-day Saint community, my child is told Black people are ugly. I see religion weaponized in a stake meeting in Seattle, where I previously lived, when my stake president counseled us to invite people who smoke, who have tattoos, and who are gay to church, and our stake Young Men president said we've been told not to associate with those types of people. I see religion weaponized when a family member decides the Church is no longer for them and family members disassociate from that person.

Religion should never be weaponized and leveraged to forcefully separate us because we are different. Religion should be, and often is, a great unifier, bringing all of God's children together to commune with our Savior, Jesus Christ.

The Gospel of Jesus Christ Is the Great Unifier

When I consider the power and influence of religion as a unifier, I think about the influence of the gospel of Jesus Christ in my life. As I shared at the beginning, I grew up in a small village in Germany. I was christened Catholic as a child. My parents always had religious materials around our home, even though we didn't attend a church regularly. I remember distinctly listening to Old Testament stories about Noah, Moses, and several ancient prophets.

When we moved to North Carolina, we attended a Southern Baptist church with my dad's family. It was invigorating and powerful, especially when Aunt Angie sang in the choir. Her soulful, heartfelt songs about Jesus Christ touched my soul. When we moved to a different neighborhood, my parents would load my siblings and me on a bus, sending us off to another church each Sunday. One year my mom's sister, Auntie Lorna, visited us and introduced us to the Jehovah's Witnesses. We fellowshipped with them for about a year, and it was a new experience for me as a nine-year-old boy. The dedication and commitment were things I had never seen before. Their civility, kindness, and focus on people was refreshing.

Then we moved to Coventry, England, in December 1990. This was my third different and distinct country, and I was only ten. This move was the distancing step away from the gospel of Jesus Christ in any form. We lived with my grandmother, and for those two years we didn't attend any church. Those two years were some of the toughest for our family, ultimately ending with us, my parents and four siblings, living in a homeless shelter. I was twelve years old and remember those days very vividly. That experience shaped much of how I see the world and especially my sisters and brothers who live in it with me.

After several months we were moved into a government housing neighborhood, where my spiritual journey would be accelerated. My father had recognized that we had been missing a religion in our lives. From the day we moved into Wood End, he started looking for a church for us. Along the way, he stumbled upon a set of sister missionaries, Sister Collins and Sister Nelson. They taught us about the gospel of Jesus Christ, a modern-day prophet, the Prophet Joseph Smith, the Book of Mormon, temples, eternal families, and how each one of us is a child of God. This additional knowledge and teaching added to the foundation I had already been given by the several other churches I had attended. Two things these sisters taught me penetrated my heart and mind: being a child of God and modern-day prophets.

For many of us as members of The Church of Jesus Christ

of Latter-day Saints, the gospel of Jesus Christ, as taught in our Church, is foundational to who we are. Our identity as a child of God is vital to our personal conversion to Him and in how we live our lives. This singular principle—being a child of God—is the great unifier in the kingdom of God. When I was taught this truth, I realized I had always known this. It was manifested in how I saw and treated my sisters and brothers in Germany, North Carolina, and, at the time, England. My young mind and heart had been shown by Heavenly Father through teachings from different religions the importance of His greatest gift: us, His children.

The Apostle Paul testified that we are all God's children: "The Spirit itself beareth witness with our spirit, that we are the children of God" (Romans 8:16).

What does it mean to us to know that each of us is a child of God? What does it teach us about our divine potential and heritage? How does this eternal truth change how we see our sisters and brothers regardless of religious beliefs, ethnic background, political views, nationality, sexual orientation, or any other attribute we wish to use to categorize each other?

Recently, President Russell M. Nelson shared the following through a social media post:

> Labels can be fun and indicate your support for any number of positive things. But if any label replaces your most important identifiers, the results can be spiritually suffocating. I believe that if the Lord were speaking to you directly, the first thing He would make sure you understand is your true identity. My dear friends, you are literally spirit children of God.

RELIGION: HOW WE USE IT MAKES A DIFFERENCE

No identifier should displace, replace, or take priority over these three enduring designations:
- Child of God
- Child of the covenant
- Disciple of Jesus Christ

Any identifier that is not compatible with those three basic designations will ultimately let you down. Make no mistake about it: Your potential is divine. With your diligent seeking, God will give you glimpses of who you may become.[4]

This eternal truth is the great unifier. No matter who we are, the choices we make, whether we stay active or not in the Church, our political views, or even our race, nothing can ever displace that we are each a child of God.

As parents, my wife and I have made this fact of divine heritage a central teaching principle in our home with our children. Wherever we've lived as a family, we've shared with our four kids that it's important not to judge others but to see them as your sisters and brothers in Heavenly Father's family.

When we live the gospel of Jesus Christ, we can be a group of people where "there were no contentions and disputations among them," with everyone "deal[ing] justly one with another" (4 Nephi 1:2). It creates an environment where we have "all things [in] common . . . ; therefore there were not rich and poor, bond and free, but they were all made free, and partakers of the heavenly gift" (v. 3).

This is the power of religion: we can see each other in the right way, as children of God, and choose to live our lives with this identifier as the main way in how we treat each other. The unifying effect of being children of God creates a connection that spans beyond this world into an eternal one, helping us to embrace each other during this mortal journey in a deeper, more Christlike way.

Discussion Questions and Personal Application

1. What is the primary purpose of the gospel of Jesus Christ in our personal lives and the world?
2. When have you seen these teachings used in a way to divide His children? What did that look like and how did it make you feel?
3. When have the tenets of the gospel of Jesus Christ been used to create division between people? Can you think of examples in your life or in your community where these tenets have been weaponized?
4. Have you used the gospel of Jesus Christ to separate yourself from others because you believed they were different? What can you do when you recognize that?
5. How is the gospel of Jesus Christ the great unifier for all Heavenly Father's children? How do the teachings of the Savior act as unifiers?
6. What examples have you seen in the scriptures, in your community, and in the world where religion has been used as a force for good? When have you witnessed the gospel unifying people who are different?
7. How does your identity as a child of God and a disciple of Jesus Christ motivate you to build unity with those around you who are different from you?
8. Who do you know who is a great example of living the gospel of Jesus Christ and unifies like the Savior in his or her interactions with others?

Some Conclusions and Some Questions

The Answer to the Question of "How": More Questions

Could the quest for greater unity pass through the simple portal of better questions and better listening? Asking the right questions is certainly one of the themes—one of the threads—that weaves itself through most of these essays, and it connects directly with the necessity of really listening.

And asking the kind of genuine questions that show respect for another view is what opens the door to still more questions, and listening, and ultimately to more understanding.

But those questions need to be more than a technique!

When questions are thought of as a method, they can become a manipulation, and can carry within them a hidden agenda. And as someone once said, "Hidden agendas are never really hidden; you can smell them like air pollution."

One young missionary told of a leader who told him that, to be effective, he had to tone down the fervor of his testimony and the aggression of his conversation. "Instead," this leader advised, "here's what you do—listen to others for a while, and ask a couple of questions, and *then* you will be able to testify and get them to commit and come to Church."

So, the missionary did—he used listening and small questions as a way to get people to like him and to pay attention to the big truths that he felt he was called there to give them.

It took this missionary a while (he wouldn't even admit how long) to realize how bad that advice was—to understand that this was a Dale Carnegie, self-help, "how to influence people" type of *technique* designed to make his manipulation of the conversation more productive. He realized that it was the opposite of real listening.

He said he forgave himself a little, looking back. After all, he was only nineteen years old, and believed that he was there as a representative of Christ's restored gospel, which he wanted desperately to share with as many people as possible and to avoid being distracted from that end. But he came to understand that he had been avoiding what he could have learned from those people he was trying so hard to teach.

He came to understand that it wasn't about who could win the "influencing" contest, or about who was right and who was wrong. He realized that there could be a win-win where both learned, both taught, and that in that atmosphere, in that *spirit*, the gospel could be grasped in deeper terms.

It was painful for him to admit, but what he'd had was an ego problem, a self-centered problem, a superiority problem, an empathy problem, a *unity* problem. He saw everything through *his* lens and was pretty sure that everyone else should too.

Could it be that all unity problems stem, at least partially, from too much ego and too little empathy, and could it be that the problem can always be solved by genuine questions and real listening?

SOME CONCLUSIONS AND SOME QUESTIONS

Disagreeing Agreeably

Harvard president Lawrence Bacow gave a speech on how to argue. He said, "Being quick to understand and slow to judge does not mean being unwilling to argue—it means arguing in a way that celebrates and strengthens our mission." He then quoted Rabbi Lord Jonathan Sacks's argument for arguing, saying we ought to argue "out of a desire to discover the truth, not out of cantankerousness or a wish to prevail over [our fellows]," not "out of envy and contentiousness and ambition for victory." When we argue for the sake of the latter, "what is at stake is not truth but power, and the result is that both sides actually suffer. If you win, I lose. But if I win, I also lose, because in diminishing you, I diminish myself. . . . The opposite is the case when the argument is for the sake of truth. If I win, I win. But if I lose, I also win—because being defeated by the truth is the only form of defeat that is also a victory." Sacks referred to this latter kind of argument as "argument for the sake of heaven."

Bacow ended with this hope: "May we all find ways to resist the lure of righteousness. To resist the lure of moral certitude. May we embrace the possibility of transcendence through argument."[1]

That kind of argument is not dismissive but respectful; it is not destructive but constructive; it is not contentious but civil; it is not of hell but of heaven.

Learning to "argue" in this way allows us to stand for what we believe without shutting off the possibility of learning something new and to engage in a dialogue where listening and speaking harmonize, and where what we hear and what we say, even if opposite, resonates rather than retaliates.

A Love of Unity

As essayists, we collectively hope that one thing this book has done is to make you appreciate more—and even love—the word *unity*.

It is a word that means tolerance.

That means understanding.

That means teamwork.

That means win-win, but when not, patient contestation.

That means mutual respect.

And it stands in opposition and in antithesis to:

Prejudice

Dissension

Animosity

Enmity

Unity is the way of our Heavenly Father and of the Lord Jesus Christ.

And it can block the way of the adversary's mode of control, force, and division.

Final Thought

In His Great Intercessory Prayer, our Lord and Savior Jesus Christ gave us a singular opportunity—to do for Him, one time, what He does for us thousands of times every day—to *listen* to and *answer* His prayer.

"That they all may be one; as thou, Father, art in me, and I in thee, that they also may be one in us" (John 17:21).

As we learn to listen, and to love, and to live in respect and empathy and mutual understanding with each other and with all of our spiritual siblings with whom we share this earth and

SOME CONCLUSIONS AND SOME QUESTIONS

this mortality, we are, in fact, bringing to pass the answer to our Lord's prayer.

And, as He always does, there in that marvelous seventeenth chapter of John, the Lord gives us a promise that will come to pass as we strive to find unity and become one. And it is a promise to cherish and never to forget: "That they might have my joy fulfilled in themselves" (v. 13).

Discussion Questions

The foreword suggested discussion as a key step in the pursuit of unity. If you do get together with others to ponder and talk about the issues of unity and diversity that these essays bring up, you may want to refer to the questions that conclude each essay. And for starters, here are some general discussion questions with reference to the whole book:

1. How have you seen division and dissension becoming a problem in the Church? Do you feel that they are more of a problem now than at other times in our history? If so, why might this be?
2. Before you started to read, did any part of you see unity and diversity as opposites or opponents? How has this perspective changed?
3. Did you finish the book more or less worried about disunity and division in the Church?
4. Which seems the bigger challenge: celebrating diversity or achieving unity? How might they be accomplished together?
5. Which essay spoke to you most meaningfully, and why?
6. With which essay did you agree most quickly? Disagree?
7. What do you feel is the root cause of disunity in the Church today?

8. Did any essay prompt you to make personal changes, either in your beliefs or your behavior? What changes?
9. What more could be done within your ward or branch to assuage division and promote unity?
10. Did you find any "how-tos" in the book—ways that you personally can become more a part of the solution than a part of the problem?

Notes

Foreword: Why Unity and Diversity Matter

1. Joseph Smith, in "Minutes, 25–26 October 1831," 11, josephsmithpapers.org; spelling standardized.
2. Henry B. Eyring, "A Priesthood Quorum," *Ensign*, November 2006.
3. Henry B. Eyring, "Our Hearts Knit as One," *Ensign*, November 2008.

Why the Lord Asks Something Beautiful and Difficult

1. C. S. Lewis, *The Great Divorce* (New York: Harper Collins, 2015).
2. Russell M. Nelson, "The Power of Spiritual Momentum," *Liahona*, May 2022.
3. Joseph Smith, in *History of the Church of Jesus Christ of Latter-day Saints*, ed. B. H. Roberts, 5:23.
4. Neal A. Maxwell, "Meeting the Challenges of Today" (Brigham Young University devotional, October 10, 1978), speeches.byu.edu.
5. Gordon B. Hinckley, "The Times in Which We Live," *Ensign*, November 2001.

Unity within the Church and Nation

1. Personal conversation with author, used by permission of Elder Wickman.
2. See Hugh W. Nibley, "Beyond Politics," byustudies.byu.edu/article/beyond-politics.
3. Patrick Mason, *Restoration: God's Call to the 21st-Century World* (Faith Matters Publishing, 2020), 63.

NOTES

4. Quoted in Peter Ackroyd, *The Life of Thomas More* (New York: Anchor Books, 1998), 405.
5. Shadi Hamid, "America Without God," *The Atlantic*, April 2021.
6. Tim Alberta, "How Politics Poisoned the Evangelical Church," *The Atlantic*, June 2022.
7. Quoted in Tad Walch, "President Nelson's yearlong call for unity," *Deseret News* (October 1, 2019).
8. Dallin H. Oaks, "Defending Our Divinely Inspired Constitution," *Liahona*, May 2021.
9. Amanda Ripley, "How to Work with Someone Who Creates Unnecessary Conflict," *Harvard Business Review*, August 2021.
10. Dallin H. Oaks, "Defending Our Divinely Inspired Constitution," *Liahona*, May 2021.
11. Quoted in Patrick Mason, *Restoration: God's Call to the 21st-Century World* (Faith Matters Publishing, 2020), 73; emphasis added.
12. Michael Gerson, "A Primer on Political Reality," Opinions, *Washington Post*, February 19, 2010; emphasis added.
13. Dallin H. Oaks, "Defending Our Divinely Inspired Constitution," *Liahona*, May 2021.

And Unity Begat Synergy

1. See David A. Bednar, "In the Strength of the Lord" (Brigham Young University devotional, October 23, 2001), speeches.byu.edu.
2. James E. Faust, "Heirs to the Kingdom of God," *Ensign*, May 1995.
3. Quoted in "Elder Uchtdorf Urges European Saints to Build Christ-Centered Unity," April 23, 2022, newsroom.ChurchofJesusChrist.org.

Rocky Ground

1. See Russell M. Nelson, "Choices for Eternity" (worldwide devotional for young adults, May 15, 2022), broadcasts.ChurchofJesusChrist.org.

NOTES

2. See Quentin L. Cook, "Prepare to Meet God," *Ensign*, May 2018.
3. Quentin L. Cook, "Hearts Knit in Righteousness and Unity," *Ensign*, November 2020.

The UNITY and Strong Families of "Nothingness"

1. See Russell M. Nelson, "Let God Prevail," *Ensign*, November 2020.
2. See *Teachings of Presidents of the Church: Harold B. Lee* (2000), 148.
3. C. S. Lewis, *Mere Christianity* (2001), 124.
4. G. K. Chesterton, *Orthodoxy* (Garden City, New York: Image Books, 1959), 20–21.

The Power of Proximity

1. Sharon Eubank, "By Union of Feeling We Obtain Power from God," *Ensign*, November 2020.
2. Bryan Stevenson, "Creating Justice," (Brigham Young University forum, October 30, 2018), https://speeches.byu.edu.

Divine Diversity

1. Boyd K. Packer, "Do Not Fear," *Ensign*, May 2004.

At-One-Ment

1. Maria Popova, "The Stoic Key to Kindness," *The Marginalian*, June 1, 2022.
2. Maria Popova, *Figuring* (New York: Pantheon, 2019).

An Optimistic Road from Contention to Unity

1. Dallin H. Oaks, "Defending Our Divinely Inspired Constitution," *Liahona*, May 2021.

Religion: How We Use It Makes a Difference

1. Gospel Topics, "Agency and Accountability," topics.ChurchofJesus Christ.org.
2. Mission of the Church, ChurchofJesusChrist.org.

NOTES

3. Quentin L. Cook, "Valiant in the Testimony of Jesus," *Ensign*, November 2016.
4. Russell M. Nelson, "Labels can be fun," Facebook, July 20, 2022.

Some Conclusions and Some Questions

1. Lawrence S. Bacow, in Jonathan Shaw, "Defeat by Truth Is Victory," *Harvard Magazine*, August 31, 2022.